STOLEN IDENTITY

Introducing Nascephobia, Nascephilia, and Maternaphilia

Thomas W. Hilgers, MD

WARNING: PORTIONS OF THIS BOOK ARE "FOR MATURE EYES ONLY"

**Library of Congress
Cataloging-in-publication-data**

Hilgers, Thomas W., – 1943 —
Thomas W. Hilgers, MD, Dip. ABOG, CFCE, SRS, SPS, AFCMSC

Includes bibliographical references and index
ISBN: 9780825310386
Ebook: 9780825309151

**Cover design, Thomas W. Hilgers, MD
Patrick Novecosky**

Layout: Matthew A. Johnson, Thomas W. Hilgers, MD

**Published in the United States of America
by: Saint Paul VI Institute Press**

In association with

**Beaufort
Books**
New York, New York

Distributed by Midpoint Trade Books
a division of Independent Publishers Group

A STAR IS BORN[1]

The right arm, forearm, and hand at time of intrauterine
surgery for spina bifida at 24 weeks gestation.

At 24 weeks, this baby had a surgical procedure to repair a spina bifida. The article, because of the spina bifida, called the scenario a "nightmare," and painted a bleak picture. But the surgery, one of the first to be done in the U.S., appeared to be helpful. She delivered at 31 weeks (premature), but the picture made her a star and gave the parents hope. (Article by Skip Hollandsworth).

1. From: Max Aguilera-Hellweg (photo), LIFE Magazine, December 1999, p. 114.

Table of Contents

Introducing Nascephobia, Nascephilia and Maternaphilia

In this book, three new terms will be introduced: **Nāscephobia**, **Nāscephilia** and **Maternaphilia**. These three terms are defined as follows:

Nāscephobia — Nascephobia is derived from the words nascent and phobia. *Nascent identifies the newly formed* and *phobia is an unrealistic fear.* Nascephobia means an unrealistic fear of a preborn baby (a nascent child). Those who zealously support abortion are **nascephobic**. Until the scourge of nascephobia is ended, we cannot legitimately say we live in a civilized society. For those who might say there is not a fear of the youngest humans, why are such drastic and violent measures promoted and conducted to remove and annihilate them? The nascent child is truly the most innocent among us.

Nāscephilia — This is the **opposite of nascephobia**. It describes a love and caring for those who are in the state of being newly formed. A **nascephiliac** is one who reaches out, supports, and loves the nascent child. With this, they will **protect the preborn**, recognizing their membership within the human race.

Maternaphilia — This has special reference to **the woman who**

is pregnant and distressed, who should be loved and cherished by those around her especially those who are close to her. However, there are many who are not close to the mother who can also exhibit support and programs out of care and concern for the mother. Programs for the women who are pregnant and distressed will be generated by those who are consistent with the principles of **maternaphilia** and opposed by those who are **nascephobic** and **maternaphobic.** These latter groups want to deny the nascent child's membership in the human race, deny them their right to live — their very existence — and deny them the love, concern and care they so desperately need.

Written by:

Russ Rooney
The author of *Be a Friend for Life (2022)*
Midwest Medical Consulting

Thomas W. Hilgers, MD, Dip ABOG,
    CFCE, SPS, SRS, AFCMSC
Clinical Professor
Creighton University School of Medicine
Senior Medical Consultant
Obstetrics, Gynecology, Reproductive
    Medicine, and Surgery
Saint Paul VI Institute
    for the Study of Human Reproduction

Introduction:
The Stolen Identity

Starting before the 1973 Supreme Court decision on abortion *(Roe v. Wade)*, the topic of abortion became very prominent. In fact, eight years following the involvement of Lawrence Lader[1] and Dr. Bernard Nathanson, the United States Supreme Court issued *Roe*. In *Roe*, **gestational age** was defined in a way scientifically and medically inaccurate and yet everybody thought, since this was coming from the United States Supreme Court, what they had to say about the issue of abortion, the unborn and pregnancy was up-to-date and accurate. Not so much!

Public opinion polls before *Roe* would ask questions like, "Should the decision to have an abortion be left up to the woman and her doctor?" This question appeared in the *Minneapolis Tribune,* a long-time liberal — not always accurate — newspaper that brought its editorial positions to the front page. When the article was read it gave the impression the majority of women were in favor of abortion, but they were only asking a question about whether the decision to have an abortion should be between the woman and her doctor. Of course, abortion being a medical/surgical procedure would involve a physician in discussion with their patient. However, the medical attitudes were changing dramatically because a **philosophical relativism** was infiltrating the medical profession. The **Hippocratic Oath** was being abandoned and was absent from many medical school graduations; when I graduated from medical school, we recited the **Declaration of Geneva** which was formulated after the Nuremberg Trials of the Nazi death camps and it said, **"I will have the utmost respect for human life from the moment of conception."** I have taken that oath very seriously while it has been abandoned in most medical schools as of this date. That type of ethical maneuver in the highest levels of medical education is one way the nascent child was **dehumanized,** and **its true identity stolen,** and this was being done under the auspices of high-level medical school academics.

Planned Parenthood in the late 1950s and early 1960s and when it first started its work, had an official position which was against abortion, but it very quickly changed its position starting in the late 1960s into the 1970s and now has become **the largest abortion provider in the United States and it has also been very profitable**. In addition, they generate over $500 million in Title X grant funds per year from the government to help support their effort. They do this, incidentally, on the shoulders of a provision in the law saying any recipient of Title X funds should **provide all methods of contraception** (including natural methods), but the providers of natural methods are often against contraception and so **it specifically excludes qualified and certified providers of natural methods** which should be a violation of the First Amendment to the United States Constitution. Nonetheless, Planned Parenthood gets away with this because they are the "voice of contraception" and, for that matter, human sexuality (even though their views on human sexuality are often retarded to say the least).

When one looks at **ultrasound technology** which began being developed in the 1960s and 1970s and taking its place in obstetrics in the late 1970s and early 1980s, it has been truly extraordinary. In the 1980s, the author had the opportunity to present a real-time ultrasound videotape in the initial stages of pregnancy to the Judiciary Committee of the United States Senate. We were extremely excited about presenting this because you could actually see the rhythmic flicker of the fetal heartbeat, but you had to be trained to be able to see it and the members of the Senate were not adequately trained to be able to see it even though we tried to point it out to them.

What is perhaps even more problematic is ultrasound itself is a technology, which has grown immensely in the last 40 years from 2-dimensional ultrasound to 3- and 4-dimensional ultrasound, from still pictures to 3-dimensional ultrasound pictures which show the baby moving, the heart beating, the thumb being sucked and so forth. It is a technology often referred to by individuals, but the only access to it is through their doctor, and then oftentimes the screen on which they can actually see the images is *hidden from view*. You do not see any television special featuring the history of ultrasound technology, the safety of it, and the extraordinary images created by today's advanced ultrasound equipment. It is like there has been a collusion suppressing these images. Even if you look at images appearing on television periodically, either through a television program or a car commercial, which shows incidentally an ultrasound photograph of a pregnant uterus, the images look like they are just blobs[2], when in fact, the ultrasound is like a camera in the womb, or as it has been called, a "window into the womb." It is really incredible, but this is all because of technological advancement, **and it has happened very rapidly**. We provide these types of services on an everyday basis in our nationally-accredited and dedicated Reproductive Ultrasound Center.

The baby is in a "hidden space" — the mother's womb, which is internal to the body — it is almost as if the baby is not in existence and as one prominent politician recently said, the heartbeat we see using ultrasound or Doppler technology is fake. At an event in 2022, Stacey Abrams, a candidate for Governor of Georgia, said, "There is no such thing as a heartbeat at six weeks. It is a manufactured sound designed to convince people that men have the right to take control of a woman's body."[3] It is hard to believe that a politician in late 2022 would be able to get away with such a statement rather than admit the technology is absolutely extraordinary and actually gives a window to the womb. It sees the nascent child (the preborn child) and it is truly extraordinary. As Medical Director of our dedicated Reproductive Ultrasound Center since 1985, I have seen all the advances occurring in ultrasound technology during this period of time and I can tell the reader that it is truly incredible and magnificent. It is not "fake" nor is it "made up," but it is truly real and **for most everyday normal people, dramatic and extraordinary!**

Have you ever seen a picture of the baby once it has been **ground up, decapitated, dismembered, burned**, or **other devastating events**

harmful to its existence? It is likely you have not seen those types of pictures, although a few people have. **The author is convinced the debate on abortion in the United States, as evidenced by the recent elections in November 2022, is a good example of a culture that does not have a realistic idea of what is happening in the abortion procedure.** Have you ever seen a description of those procedures? I know that you have heard empty slogans like, "My body … my choice!" But that is not a true indication of what is actually happening.

Lila Rose, the foundress of **Live Action** recently wrote: "Millions of Americans simply do not know the dark truth about the killing of preborn children in our country, much like many Americans did not know or turned a blind eye towards the injustice and violence of Jim Crow ... Most people — especially young Americans — have no clue just how violent, cruel, and barbaric abortion really is ..."[4]

What about the **role of women** as a **protector of their unborn child?** They have been in denial of their role as a protector and provider of nourishment. Men also deny their responsibilities as protectors, but often, it is done because of their own selfish reasons, not to be involved in the birth of these babies, which are often in unwed mothers. The men have certain supportive responsibilities held true over many hundreds of years, and they want to avoid those responsibilities.

The **"Culture of Life"** has really become a **"Culture of Death"** and its anti-child sentiments have become the norm. When President Biden makes fun of the conservatives, it is absolutely clear he does not share the desire to make America great again. Mass media go along with this denial (particularly television, newspapers, and other periodicals). It is also commonly seen on the Internet. But the radio seems to be different in its approach and often discusses the abortion issue in more realistic terms, though even at that, the description provided is often not complete and real.

So, the question comes about, **"Have you ever seen the outcome of an abortion?"** People have said this is too dramatic, too real and too disgusting, showing blood and gore in a way we humans are not used to looking at (if we are not doctors). What about lawsuits against the doctors who perform abortions and completely separating a living human being from the mother, destroying its existence and, of course, its future? These are all real!

It is unfortunately true, however, during the course of these last

40+ years, the true identity of **what is growing within the womb has been "stolen."** There has been a **purposeful dehumanization** of **human life** *in utero* to keep the public from appreciating what really is. This is tragic, and this book tries to teach the reader about the real identity of this baby *in utero*, the reality of its growth and development *in utero*, to realize **the human zygote** is the **single most important cell of the human being**. It is responsible for the growth, development, and maturing of the **entire human life spectrum beginning with the human zygote and concluding with natural death later in life, usually after birth with a lifespan of 76 years for men and 82 years for women.** If you come into reading this book with the idea there is no identity to the nascent child — in other words, you believe what you have been taught all of these years by mostly the **mainstream media, television, newspapers, occasional reality reporting, then this book will shine a light on all of this for each one of you. It is an important light and one needing to be taken seriously**!

Let there be no doubt that politicians and mass media have kept the true and real identity of this new life and the violent and ugly images of its destruction away from the people, and it has been purposeful! The true identity **has been stolen** by **preborn human life deniers!** This book hopes to educate its readers so they can **better appreciate the extraordinary events that have occurred to each one of us!**

"Planned Parenthood and other pro-abortion groups have **masked abortion in euphemisms** (emphasis applied). Instead of saying abortion is a violent act that destroys the life of a child, they say they are simply 'terminating the pregnancy' or removing a 'clump of cells' and the growing baby inside the womb is only referred to as the 'product of conception' ... **the abortion industry thrives on misinformation and covering up the truth** (emphasis applied). Planned Parenthood knows that if women could see what abortion really is and looks like, more mothers would choose life for their babies."[4]

If there are **climate deniers** and **election deniers** there also are **human life deniers,** and, with the latter, we have gone far beyond any other extermination event in human history! And the preborn child is **entirely innocent** and, because of unrealistic fears, is being **tortured, ground up,** and **decapitated** in its own clean and sterile **termination camps**. They are conducted by those who are cold to the problems present with whom they do not wish to become involved. Those who **deny life** and **deny the needs of the mothers are part of the problem! There is a need to discard their role as a part of the problem in order to become part of the solution!**

"Not long after the Civil Rights Movement began … Rosa Parks sat down on a seat right at the front of a Montgomery city bus and refused to get up and move to the back of the bus for anyone."[4] The **disinformation that has been associated with the pro-abortion movement has truly been overwhelming.** Now, while *Dobbs v. Mississippi* has reversed *Roe v. Wade,* the status of the pre-born child has still not been completely decided states throughout the country are looking at laws in their state legislative bodies that would allow abortion at 15 weeks or less, or some other arbitrary timeline. In fact, in our own legislature (Nebraska), two pro-abortion senators have been working on ways to again legalize abortion in our state. Many years ago, these were called Jim Crow laws. Now, we have moved to what could be called, "Baby-X Laws (see page 131)." **The injustice continues!**

1. Hilgers T.W.: The Fake and Deceptive Science Behind Roe v. Wade. Who are Lawrence Lader, Dr. Bernard Nathanson, and Cyrus Vance? Saint Paul VI Institute Press. Omaha, Nebraska, USA, 2020.

2. While good ultrasound images of the nascent child can be seen, and the images are somewhat better (see TV ads for Amica and Edward Jones), 3-D and 4-D images are rarely available to the general public.

3. Fox News. Twitter users baffled after Stacey Abrams claims no fetal heartbeat at six weeks: 'Wild conspiracy theory'. Published September 22, 2022. Accessed January 20, 2023. https://www. foxnews.com/media/twitter-users-baffled-stacey-abrams-claims-no-fetal-heartbeat-six-weeks-wild-conspiracy-theory

4. Lila Rose, President of"Live Action" in a letter to supporters, March, 2023.

Chapter 1

The Termination of the Innocents

I have been taking care of pregnant women and delivered their babies for more than 40 years. I have also been interested in the various life issues for many years when looking at the devastating holocaust of the Nazis towards Jewish people (and others) during the course of World War II. One question that I have had from early on was "Why did it happen?" How does something like that happen? What kind of a **derangement** would lead to something like this or are we humans just so weak we do not speak up at the appropriate time. I am German by my heritage. Our family came to the United States about four generations ago. I am truly American, but I had to wonder if there was not something in my genetics making something like this occur more easily.

I wanted to know whether it was a weakness of the German (or Northern European) heritage I inherited or was it something else. So, I made a pledge to myself and to God as best I could, I would speak up and I would not be persuaded to remain quiet when the abortion issue came along.

In abortion, we have had in the United States the loss of more than 60 million nascent children (preborn children) since the widespread legalization of abortion with the Supreme Court decision *Roe v. Wade*. We can not and should not ever use the term *holocaust* to describe any event ending in the wanton destruction of a broad category of human beings unless it is related to the holocaust in Nazi Germany or a nuclear holocaust. However, at the same time, we cannot let that go by giving our silent ascent to it. **Being silent is the same thing as giving it one's approval.** Of course, that is not entirely correct, and I am aware of that, but at the same time, so much of this has gone on because of two major forces in our culture. This stems from a political and media voice, ultimately godless, and guides an ever-expanding conglomerate of news sources. These news sources are often driven by a corporate financial support structure increasingly becoming more godless in its own right.

One of the things I have learned is that it is not a good idea to bring God into this equation because it only suggests the voice that is speaking is a religious one. But while religions may direct some of these comments, the everyday mission of the religious perspective is carried out by those who are believers. This is a direction, incidentally, that is more and more perceived by those who think religious belief is right next to superstition; those who promote the "belief" that super-stition and religious belief belong in the same category, know virtually nothing about religion. I should point out, this is not a book about religion, specifically, but about **trying to get to truth … truth that matters!**

While you should not use the term "holocaust" when you look at 60 million lives of real human beings **violently and viciously destroyed with abortion**, it is now more than 10 times the numbers associated with abortion than it is with the holocaust, and, **yet, it is like we have no sense of what is happening to us as a nation.**

There are, however, reasons for why all of this has happened, and there can also be reasons why we begin to adopt the science that has informed us otherwise — in spades — that these are individual human lives we are destroying.

For example, **how many lives have been destroyed and how many**

real problems have been solved? While a lot of research has tried to establish various components of this issue, one of the major issues not studied has been an assessment of what problems have been solved and what problems have been perpetuated or inaugurated as a result of the proposed solution, which, in our current culture, is abortion!

In my medical practice, I have been the Director of an Advanced Ultrasound Program with 3- and 4-dimensional real-time obstetrical ultrasound services and we have had the opportunity to study the nascent child in a way unheard of in decades gone by. It is truly impressive, and, yet, we have radiology departments and offices with obstetricians/gynecologists who have ultrasound equipment, who, when they perform an ultrasound on a pregnant woman, turn the television screen in a different direction so the woman cannot see what the technician sees. This is usually done by command from those who are in administrative charge of these types of programs. At our place, we have a television that is well within the range of viewing for the women and their spouses and they are able to see what we see. You will see some of those pictures in this book.

If you look at the history of the abortion debate, you will find that, early on, even before abortion was legalized, the true identity of the nascent child was kept from the public, and we are now 50 years since *Roe v. Wade* and still doing that. Ultrasound, which has this incredible ability to see into the womb in a way that we have never been able to see before, proves, beyond a doubt, that these are little human beings, alive, moving and actually very vibrant young children. And, yet, we as a culture and society, do not seem to care about that. They do not seem to realize the people who could solve some of the major problems we are confronted with in the world, have been aborted (killed). Some of the great discoveries have not been made because we have aborted the individual who might be able to make that discovery. We have no thought really about what we are doing to our future, which includes, incidentally, a philosophy and public policy approach **including lethalism as one of its primary solutions**. We have **stolen the true identity of these children** and **we continue to lie about it;** if there is anything religion teaches us in all of this, it is that **we should not lie. We should tell the truth; we should reflect the truth, and we should follow a path of truth!** That is what this book is about, and I am anxious for it to be released so that it can truly increase the impact of truth. **These 60 million plus lives MATTER**!!! We cannot continue to deceive ourselves; we will not get away with it. It will all come back to haunt us and the question will be raised sometime in the future, "Was there something in the genetic makeup of the American people (and for that matter much of Western Europe and many nations of the world) preventing us from seeing the reality of what it is we are doing and avoiding the solutions before us?"

Keep in mind, the nascent child is a completely innocent human being whose life is being **terminated without a trial.** The termination is by **dismemberment, scalding, suctioning of its brain** in an **ugly, violent** and **vicious** death. Much has been written about **fetal pain** but there is **another type of pain** without much attention given to it. This is the **pain and emotional agony** and **sense of loss** occurring **when people see the pictures of the aborted child** similar to the ones shown in this book. Pro-life advocates have shown pictures like these before but have become fearful of the painful reaction they produce in viewers. It is similar to the holocaust images — they, too, are painful to see. **Man's inhumanity to man! This pain is real. The termination of the Innocents is real and truly ugly to see!**

Chapter 2

The Biochemical Identifier

Human life is a spectrum of human life events — continuously growing, developing, growing up, maturing, aging and eventually dying. If any one of these is significant or valuable, then each step along the way is also valuable. If one of these steps is removed, then the whole spectrum is removed. **If each stage shares the same biochemical identifier**[1] — used extensively in American jurisprudence as a definitive identifier — **then all linking up to that identity are also significant, unless, of course, that identity has been hidden or stolen, purposely or without purpose.**

In the **United States Constitution**, it is often said the nascent child (the preborn child) is not mentioned. In *Roe v. Wade*, for example, the nascent child is not considered to be a "person" in the Constitutional sense (since it is said that the nascent child is not thought to be mentioned). Those who claim this location in "the spectrum" are denied personhood. (Incidentally, this would not be the first time that the Supreme Court has excluded certain human beings within "the spectrum" to not be a human person.) But, **the nascent child is** mentioned in the Preamble to the United States Constitution in a way which would include all members of "the spectrum" who would be recipients of the rights expressed in the Bill of Rights of the United States Constitution.

The Preamble to the United States Constitution Includes All Future Generations[1]

The Preamble states:

> "*We the People* of the United States, in order to form a more perfect Union, establish Justice, ensure domestic Tranquility, provide for the common Defense, promote the general welfare and secure the blessings of liberty to ourselves and our *posterity* (emphasis applied), do ordain and establish this Constitution of the United States[1]

The biochemical identified which is a life-long marker that stays with "the spectrum" of everyone's life is **the individual's DNA type,**[2] **the identifier** present throughout the entire spectrum of one's life through natural death. It is more accurate than one's fingerprints present from the sixth to the eighth week after conception. DNA typing frequently replaces fingerprints in today's world with these newer biotechniques for their measurement, making it easier and more accurate. The word *posterity* means "future generations" (Webster's II New College Dictionary).

---

1. The United States Constitution. https://www.archives.gov/founding-docs/constitution-transcript. Accessed January 24, 2023.

2. DNA typing has been done as early as 16–20 weeks gestation using cells from the nascent child, and should be there from conception. From: DNA Typing. *Encyclopedia.com,* October 10, 2022.

Chapter 3

Nascephobia vs. "The Adjustment"

The first and foremost **alternative to abortion** is to help pregnant women realize they are not alone in their pregnancy, and they will be supported during the course of that pregnancy. There is an **"adjustment reaction"** human beings go through when something major happens in their life. These adjustments are often emotional on the one hand, while, on the other hand, they are associated with some degree of physical symptoms. It is true, for example, when you become pregnant, you not only have a small child within your body (womb), but the adjustment needs to be made associated with both the short- and long-term responsibilities with being a mother or a father. **Obviously men and women adjust to these things differently.** Because the woman has physical symptoms associated with the pregnancy, it makes a lot of sense she would be more impacted — at least physically and externally — than the father. **The adjustments men go through are different** because they are distant from it to a certain degree, and it is hard for them to understand it all since they have never themselves gone through it. In fact, little has been done to better understand it.

Incidentally, there has been this idea floating around that men can become pregnant. **It is the kind of thing in our culture that creates needless confusion. Men CANNOT become pregnant! It is physiologically impossible.** And yet, there is this controversy within the culture saying **men can become pregnant** because it is promoted by a widespread communications network supported by corporate entities with dollar signs associated with them and who do not always have the truth as a focus.

Some people will say they agree a man cannot become pregnant, but just wait until a uterus, tubes and ovaries can be transplanted into the man's body; then he will be able to become a mother. One huge problem with this is the male pelvic structure is different than the female's pelvic structure. **The pelvic structure of women is actually designed to have babies, whereas the pelvic structure of men is not.** If for some reason a man would get pregnant and reach full term, **he would, almost for certain, need to have a cesarean section; there is no efficient birth canal to speak of.** In other words, it is **a really ludicrous idea,** and we waste time in our culture with these types of ludicrous ideas.

The word **nascephobia** refers to the fear of the nascent child (the child in the womb). The woman can have a good deal of fear and "trembling" when she becomes pregnant. The **adjustment reaction** she goes through is an important one and a very positive one most of the time. It is an adjustment reaction we all go through when we are confronted with what could be considered a life-changing component of who we are. Our plans may change, even if the pregnancy ends in miscarriage, there are emotional sequelae occurring. And just as that woman at that time needs emotional support, in all of these adjustments, **emotional support is necessary.** Husbands — men — on the other hand, often do not know exactly how to do that or even its importance, but it is extremely important and it is vital, frankly, as they must become active participants. We, as a medical profession, I might point out, are doing a horrible job of bringing men into this or, for that matter, providing support of their own.

As an example of this, many years ago, there were really good classes for women who were pregnant — which usually involved couple participation — to learn about pregnancy, labor and delivery. Knowledge helps reduce the level of the reaction to being pregnant and whatever fear there may be of childbirth, but it also provides support to the pregnant woman, as well as her husband, or others who may be the woman's primary support, when she goes into labor. It is always good to remind a pregnant woman that there have been billions of women who have gone through this before, and especially in our modern world, they survive and often will survive as better people because of what they went through to give birth to their child. Their marriages can become stronger; their resolve to be the mother of this child becomes bonded (maternal infant bonding) and it is really, really impressive. Having said that, however, the medical profession has almost been a detraction to all of this. The point I am trying to **bring across** is that some pain and suffering which most of us do not want, can actually be positive and make us stronger people.

Nascephobia, which is a **fear of the child in the womb** can be resolved by how we deal with "the adjustment reaction" occurring in the early stages of pregnancy. Incidentally, **this is occurring at the same time the woman is in some ways pushed to have an abortion and is very vulnerable. Most abortions occur in the first trimester of pregnancy when this adjustment is most prominent.** The pressures occurring relative to this adjustment is important to all women and to all mothers and fathers, and, yet, we treat it as a profession like it is not important — it really has nothing to do with our medical expertise — it has nothing to do with anything important to the health and welfare of the mother, the father or the family.

I do need to tell you that in the training of young obstetrician/gynecologists, there is virtually nothing provided to them that dealing directly with the emotional support necessary to a woman who is pregnant and going through this type of an adjustment — which is otherwise completely normal and natural — or in other situations, such as a woman who might have had a miscarriage or is going through a miscarriage or, unfortunately, a stillborn baby, or a baby born with a defect. All of these things challenge our ability to provide support, and it often starts in the doctor's office and, unfortunately, ends there because the doctor does not know what to do. They all think everybody wants simple, easy solutions, and, yet, abortion is neither simple nor easy and has its own set of short- and long-term problems associated with it (which most medical doctors seem to deny).

So, we need to recognize the fear of this child is, to some extent, normal, and it is one reason why pregnancy is nine months in duration, which helps not only the woman but also her spouse go through some of these adjustment reactions, which are otherwise normal but can become unhealthy when they are not dealt with in a positive way.

Chapter 4

A Picture Dictionary of the Essence that is the Human Existence

Introduction

Across the last several years, technology has advanced, allowing us to **observe the growth and development of the nascent child** in ways we have not been able to in the past. The very first ultrasound videotape we produced was presented to a special Senate committee in the early 1980s for consideration. At the time, I made the comment that the **advances in ultrasound technology** would expect to be incredible over the next several years. Having made that comment, I have been impressed *beyond my ability to see* what has actually happened.

If you look at the ability to observe the young child as it grows within its mother's womb, it has exceeded just about everybody's expectations. And, yet, for the most part, the advances have gone unnoticed. While true, patients have benefitted significantly from our ability to have access to direct observation of the young child in the womb, it has grown enormously over these years with ultrasound being only one modality. **Special cameras** have been developed that can take video pictures of the baby in the uterus through a small incision in the uterus, and the moving pictures of this have been released to the public.[1] Ultrasound technology itself has gone from a somewhat blurry two-dimensional scan to real-time motion picture ultrasound, to what now is 3-dimensional and 4-dimensional ultrasound in real-time. Three-dimensional ultrasound is like taking a Smart-phone photograph of the baby while still in the uterus without any incisions or insertion of instruments directly into the baby's space.

And, yet, these images have never been used to their fullest capability. While video pictures of the baby *in utero* have been taken, along with still photographs, the full capacity of the educational component of those images has not come close to its full capability. With ultrasound technology, there have been greater advances in this particular field than almost any field of medical imaging, and yet, **when have you seen a special program on national television exploring the dynamics of 3-D and 4-D ultrasound imaging?** In fact, it has actually gone in the opposite direction. Many imaging centers, which are coordinated by radiologists and obstetricians, often have policies where imaging of the baby in 3- and 4-dimensional ultrasound is specifically prohibited from showing the patient (the mother and the father) so they do not see the images that the sonographer sees. While some videotape of the ultrasound study was initially given to the patients so they would have a visual remembrance of their baby while it was in its first home, policies were implemented to abolish this practice. As a result, **an enormously positive educational tool** has been kept from patients. Even when ultrasound is shown on national television, for example, in a commercial presentation of some sort, the ultrasound image often looks like "a blob" and does not give the full value of the image to the observer.

At the **Saint Paul VI Institute, we have a dedicated reproductive ultrasound imaging center** which, during the course of its life span (now 38 years), has shared these images with patients beginning with still photographs (which is all that we had at the time), and then later video of 3- and 4-dimensional ultrasound images. In the late 1990s, we received **national accreditation by the American Institute of Ultrasound in Medicine** after making application for this accreditation by the submission of an application form which included a variety of different images. This accreditation has been in continuation since, and **we were the first imaging center in our state to receive this national accreditation at the time it became available.**

Since, we have shared with patients these images and have even provided video images at various times to the mothers and the fathers. Of course, it has been extraordinary to be able to share these images with patients, and their reactions have been profound.

This chapter reveals the imaging that we have documented by the use of 3- and 4-dimensional ultrasound, direct color photography of some of the images we see at the earlier stages of life, along with some images artistically drawn by the Queen's own physician and published over 200 years ago[2]. In fact, while this is a still photograph presentation for the most part, there is one color photograph of a heart beating at about 120 beats per minute from a nascent child at approximately 30 days post-conception. This is available on the internet (for the last couple of years) at www.knowreality.us and more recently on the Internet at www.womanlifechoice.com. These images show **objectively**, using an ultrasound technology which is available at the most advanced levels and **reveals (in an objective and absolutely clear-cut way) that human existence is a spectrum beginning with conception (the human zygote) and culminating with graduation to the extracorporeal existence of this new human being. These images need to be taken seriously! We are in the midst of what has become the most critical human rights issue in current existence.** If we can kill and dismember the nascent child while still in the uterus, then we can deny the existence of anyone along the life spectrum — the essence of the human being! **Enlightenment must come to our culture and people cannot be afraid (nascephobic) of what our creative capabilities are nor the extraordinary beauty of this creation.**

Human life, to be accurate, needs to be considered as a **spectrum of life** moving from one stage to another — **most of the stages look different one from the other — but they are no less human at each and every stage. We all started as a human zygote, progressed to an embryo, then a fetus, then through the birthing process, an infant, child, teenager, adolescent, young adult, adult, middle age, old age and then death (all natural events). At each stage, the DNA typing (the identifier) is the same, but individual for each.**

In the next several pages, the appearance, and in some cases, the movement of the new human is shown including a heartbeat at 4+ weeks. These early developments or stages of life have been experienced by all of us, although our memory is limited. If we have value now, we had value at all of these stages and political types cannot and should not reconfigure these life stages in a way becoming politically suitable to them. In fact, religions may have "different definitions" relative to the "entire spectrum of human life," **but science must propel us to its common ground!**

In Chapter 5, I will present some pictures from the animal world for everyone to identify. In Chapter 6, actual pictures of induced abortions will also be presented. **It is more horrific than your mind can even imagine and is "for mature eyes only!"**

In order to discuss this in the future, "the entire spectrum of human life" (from the beginning until its natural end), **the entire "circle of life" must be respected, protected and identified with their natural (and normal) differences.**

The only solution that makes sense in a pluralistic society for **direct abortion** is one life (the mother) v. the life of the nascent child, but in over 45 years of delivering thousands of babies, taking care of pregnant women during their pregnancies and treating literally thousands of couples with infertility and/or repetitive miscarriage, **I have never seen a woman die in pregnancy or childbirth.** We do not need to express and/or believe untrue statements related to pregnancy-related events. All stages may look different from the others. Those who are pro-abortion know this and use words and phrases to "slice and dice" human beings into separate entities so they can eliminate whichever part of "the spectrum" they would like at any point in time.

So, just defining the target group out of existence because they look or act differently is completely inappropriate and is an example of a deranged thought process. It is the nascent child (pre-born child) that this book deals with, but it could be racial (e.g., Blacks and the Dred Scott decision or Jews during the Nazi era of Adolph Hitler's regime or White, Christian people who were the target of Josef Stalin), Asians (during Mao Tse-Tung's reign in China) or the massive annihilation of more than 1 million people in Cambodia. It goes on and on and included Catholics, Muslims, Protestants, and others.

Over the many years of the abortion debate, the true identity of the nascent child has **been stolen** with the use of **completely inaccurate** terms and phrases and put into a different context, which is **dehumanizing** — using such words as "a few blobs of protoplasm" or a "non-viable baby," etc., etc.

These words have been used on purpose to **dehumanize the nascent child**, much of what had been done in other eras to fool the general public into thinking that **human life was not human!** They say it does not "look human" because of its early physical appearance, which makes it look different than more mature forms of "the spectrum of life." **A lot of it has to do with political nomenclature being used instead of nomenclature reflecting reality!** ■

1. The Biology of Prenatal Development. Produced by the Endowment for Human Development, 2006, www.ehd.org.

2. All embryological drawings in this book are from: Hunter W: Physician Extraordinary to the Queen, Professor of Anatomy in the Royal Academy, and Fellow of the Royal and Antiquarian Societies, originally published in 1774. The Special Edition of the Anatomy of the Human Gravid Uterus Exhibited in Figures. Privately printed for the members of the Classics of Obstetrics & Gynecology Library. 1991, A Division of Gryphon Editions, PO Box 531210, Birmingham, Alabama 35253 USA. Originally published by Birmingham by John Baskerville, 1774.

FIGURE 4-1

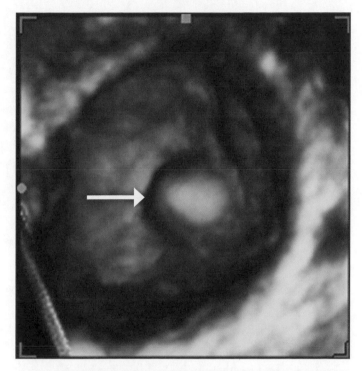

A 3D ULTRASOUND PHOTOGRAPH OF THE CUMULUS OOPHERUS (AT ARROW) JUST BEFORE OVULATION[1]. THE CUMULUS OOPHERUS CONTAINS THE OVUM (EGG) FROM THE MOTHER, BUT IS NOT A HUMAN BEING.

1. First presented by the Saint Paul VI Institute at the National Meeting of the American Institute for Ultrasound in Medicine (AIUM), New York, 2014.

FIGURE 4-2A

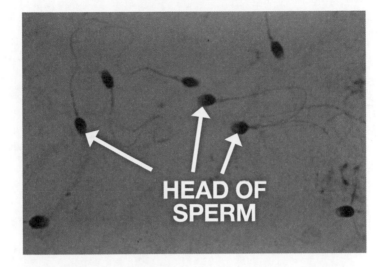

Human sperm, which contain the father's genetic contribution to the nascent child has 23 chromosomes located in **the head of the sperm** (see arrows). These are human sperm, but **not** human beings.

FIGURE 4-2B[1]

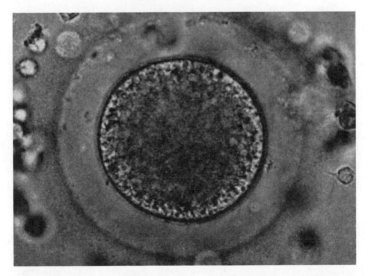

A human ovum (egg), which contains the mother's genetic contribution to the nascent child. This also has 23 chromosomes located in the nucleus of the ovum. This ovum is from a human female, but it is **not** a human being.

1. From Hartman C: Science and the safe period, 1962

MOMENTS BEFORE CONCEPTION

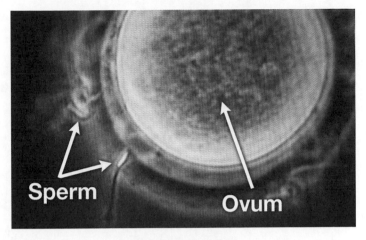

FIGURE 4-3A[1]

The egg (ovum) and sperm both have a limited life span. The ovum, once released from the mother's ovary, dies 12–24 hours later. The sperm lives for 8–9 days, but it is capable of fertilizing the ovum for a maximum of only 3–5 days.

Many people have been led to believe we are just a grown up sperm or a grown up egg. But we are not!

The sperm in this photo (4-3B) is about to enter the ovum.

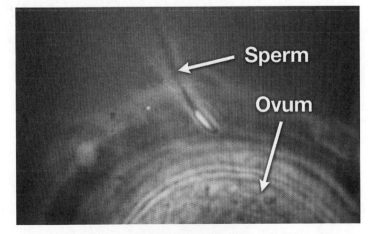

FIGURE 4-3B[1]

1. Pictures from: Blandeau R: Personal Communication

FIGURE 4-4
THE MOMENT OF CONCEPTION
THE ESTABLISHMENT OF THE HUMAN ZYGOTE
AND THE BEGINNING OF A HUMAN LIFE

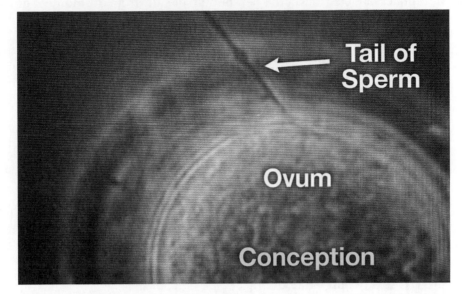

The tail of the sperm is visible but outside the ovum. The head of the sperm that contains 50% of the chromosomal compliment of the new human person is now **inside** the ovum. In 15–30 minutes, it joins with the other 50% of the chromosomes contributed by the ovum. This is the ***moment of conception*** with an average lifespan of about 76 years for males and 82 years for females.

This is the **Human Zygote,** and it is the **single most potent and important cell** in the existence of a human being. A new DNA type is created with union of these gametes. **It creates a new 46 chromosome human identity.** This exists from this moment **throughout the spectrum that is its human existence.**

In a recently published poll there were a large majority of participants (all biologists) who consistently **affirmed the view that life begins at conception** (fertilization) (**96.8%**; 1,011 out of 1,044) than those who **consistently rejected the concept that life began at conception** (fertilization) (**3.2%**; 33 out of 1,044).[1]

1. Jacobs, Steven Andrew: The Scientific Consensus on When a Human's Life Begins, Issues in Law and Medicine, 36:221-233, Fall 2021. (Professor Jacobs graduated from the Northwestern University School of Law in 2016 with his JD and in 2019 from the University of Chicago with his PhD).

THE SINGLE MOST IMPORTANT
HUMAN CELL (SMIHC)

The relatively new science of **DNA typing**[1] could possibly distinguish the unique characteristics of this new human literally from the **moment of conception**. *In vitro* fertilization, while it dehumanizes the early human person because it is such a highly abortive technology, does prove **without a doubt** that a new individual human life begins when the sperm and egg unite. No IVF babies have been born where this event has been skipped. The *human zygote* **is an extraordinary cell with capabilities beyond all other cells in the human body because it is programmed to be so absolutely essential to the ongoing growth and development of the new human person.** Many refer to this as *potential human life,* and, yet, there is nothing "potential" about it. **It is actual human life! It is human life WITH potential!**

The *human zygote* is the *single most important human cell* **(SMIHC)!** *It is a cell that precedes all stem cells.* It is the *originating cell* of each individual human life with extraordinary capabilities! **We all started with this cell, and if our lives have any value now, the SMIHC surely had value then.**

Many people like to say this is a "belief." By putting it into the context of a belief, it is made to seem like one has to have a special faith to be able to see the unborn in its reality. And yet, none of that is true. **This is a scientific observation — objective, species specific, reproducible and enlightened!** We have made *a gross error* as a nation and a culture in denying it.

In the abortion issue, the conflict exists because it is a public policy issue ultimately revolving around the fight to **protect this new human's right to live!** Others want to protect their "right" to sexual intercourse at any time and/or any place without recourse to basic responsibilities. **This latter view has become a religion to many, with abortion as one of its "sacraments," and, in doing so it could be seen as a violation of the First Amendment to the U.S. Constitution.** It is a violation of a major foundational principle of the nation. Each **Human Zygote** is a new, **completely human identity**, which might also be identified through specific **DNA typing**.

---

1. DNA typing has been done as early as 16–20 weeks gestation using cells from the nascent child, and should be there from conception. From: DNA Typing. *Encyclopedia.com*, October 10, 2022.

FIGURE 4-5[1]

After the sperm has entered the ovum, the two nuclei are seen as they approach each other. They are properly referred to as pronuclei.

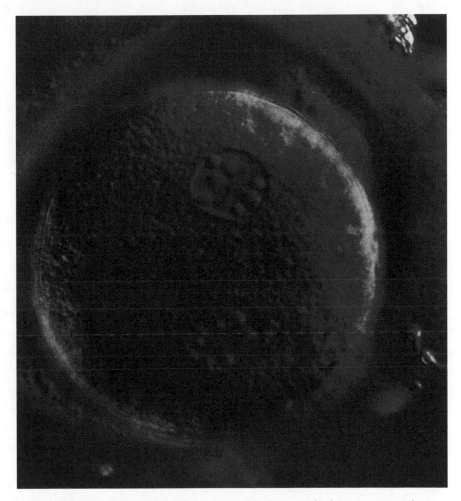

The pronuclei are not yet joined, so this is a prelude to conception.

1. From: LIFE Magazine, The First Picture Ever of Life (Human) Begins, Lennart Nilsson, Photographer, August 1990, p. 30.

FIGURE 4-6[1]

The pronuclei are about to merge. After they merge, fertilization (also called conception) has occurred, and a **human zygote** (a single cell human being) is formed (initiated).

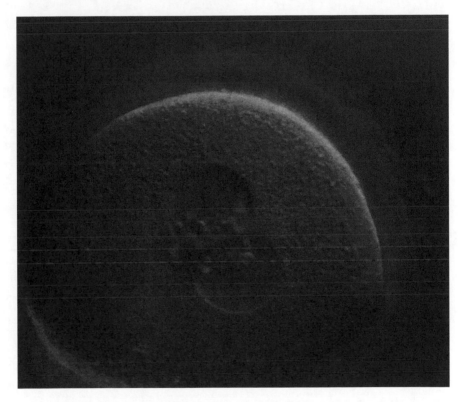

1. From: LIFE Magazine, The First Picture Ever of Life (Human) Begins, Lennart Nilsson, Photographer, August 1990, p. 30.

FIGURE 4-7[1]

This photo is taken after the first cell division. The human zygote continued forward in its human development with this two cell stage.

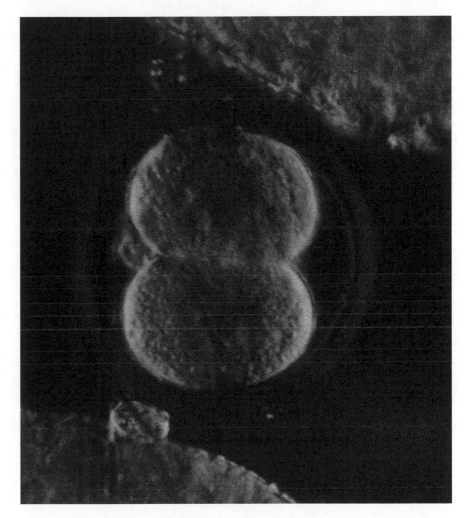

1. From: LIFE Magazine, The First Picture Ever of Life (Human) Begins, Lennart Nilsson, Photographer, August 1990, p. 31.

FIGURE 4-8[1]

THE NASCENT HUMAN BEING AT 8 DAYS
FOLLOWING CONCEPTION

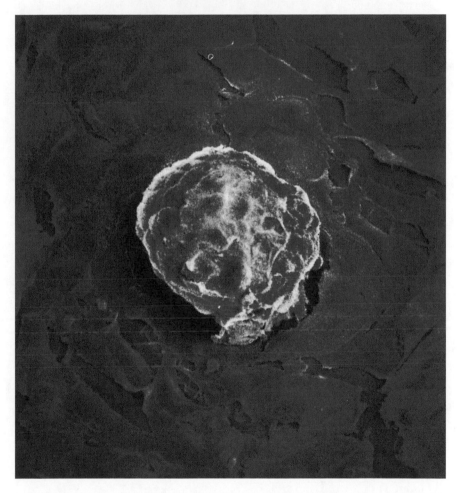

1. From: LIFE Magazine, The First Picture Ever of Life (Human) Begins, Lennart Nilsson, Photographer, August 1990, p. 37.

FIGURE 4-9[1]

DEVELOPMENT OF THE HUMAN EYE FROM 5 TO 6.5 WEEKS GESTATIONAL AGE[2]

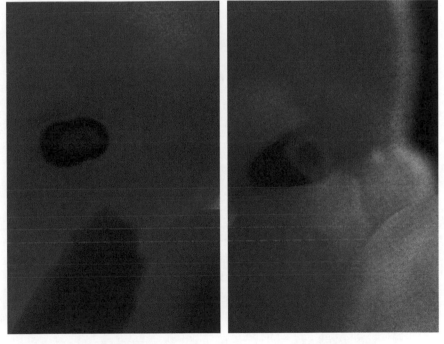

5 WEEKS   **6.5 WEEKS**

1. From: LIFE Magazine, The First Picture Ever of Life (Human) Begins, Lennart Nilsson, Photographer, August 1990, p. 42.

2. Gestational age is always two weeks longer than fetal age (see glossary).

FIGURE 4-10

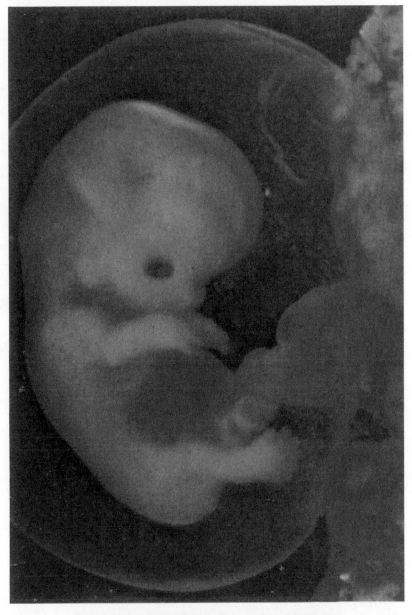

THE NASCENT CHILD AT 6 WEEKS (EST.) OF GESTATIONAL AGE.*

*From: Hilgers TW, Horan DJ: Abortion and
Social Justice, Sheed & Ward, New York, 1972

FIGURE 4-11A

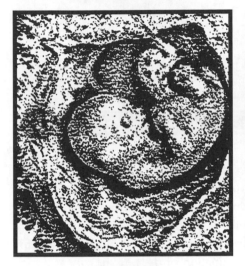

HUNTER[1]
1774
6-7 WEEKS

FIGURE 4-11B

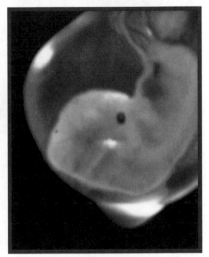

HILGERS
1970s
6-7 WEEKS

Figure 4-11A & 4-11B: On the left is a copy of the original drawing of the embryo at 6–7 weeks published by Dr. William Hunter, the Queen's physician, in 1774[1]. On the right is an actual color photo of an embryo at a similar age, but taken in the 1970s. This reveals the embryonic presence was known for 200 years before *Roe* and explains why the right to live was the public policy position for so long before *Roe* (see *Dobbs v. Jackson,* 2022). (Photo: Thomas W. Hilgers, MD).

1. All embryological drawings in this book are from: Hunter W: Physician Extraordinary to the Queen, Professor of Anatomy in the Royal Academy, and Fellow of the Royal and Antiquarian Societies, originally published in 1774. The Special Edition of the Anatomy of the Human Gravid Uterus Exhibited in Figures. Privately printed for the members of the Classics of Obstetrics & Gynecology Library. 1991, A Division of Gryphon Editions, PO Box 531210, Birmingham, Alabama 35253 USA. Originally published by Birmingham by John Baskerville, 1774.

FIGURE 4-12A

FETAL HEARTBEAT AS IDENTIFIED USING ULTRASOUND TECHNOLOGY

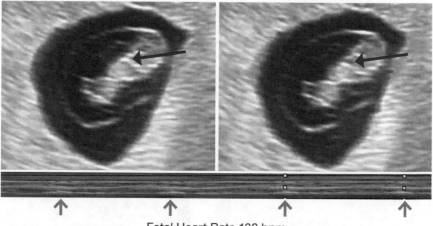

Fetal Heart Rate 138 bpm

The two images above are less than 0.5 seconds apart from each other. On the left-hand side, the heart is closed as the blood has just been released from it. On the right-hand side, there is a darkened area measuring only a few millimeters, but **that darkened area is a blood chamber within the fetal heart** which fills up in anticipation of the next heartbeat. Once the heart contracts, then that pushes the blood out from the heart into the blood vessels which are not shown. So if you use your eyes and go back and forth left to right, right to left from the image on the left and the image on the right, you'll see that there is an emptying of the heart chamber between the chamber on the right and the one on the left (see red arrows). In a real-time ultrasound image where the motion of the heart is also identified, you can see the heart emptying its blood-filled chamber from the right side (above) and then the image on the left is empty and it fills up again. This is readily apparent on real-time ultrasound which is motion picture-like ultrasound imaging. Such an image is present on the internet at <u>www. womenlifechoice.com</u>. The image on p. 39 which is identified as Figure 4-12 is **an actual color video** of the four chambers of the heart at approximately 30 days of pregnancy (this would be 4 weeks and 2 days fetal age and 6 weeks and 2 days gestational age). The image was taken from an early embryo that had to be removed because it was caught in the fallopian tube (an ectopic pregnancy — which occurs in about 1% of pregnancies).

FIGURE 4-12

THE HEARTBEAT AT 6.5 WEEKS GESTATIONAL AGE
4.5 WEEKS FETAL AGE

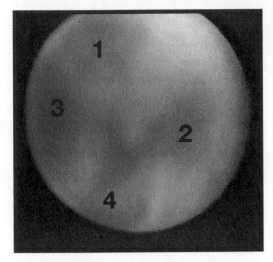

Figure 4-12: A color picture of an embryo's 4-chamber heart at 30–35 days post-conception. Live action of this heartbeat is on the video freely available at ***www.womanlifechoice.com***. The embryo's heartbeat is 120 beats per minute, contrasted to the maternal heartbeat, which averages 72 beats per minute, consistent with the normal heartbeats of two separate persons. The four chambers of the heart are also identified.

Another attempt to steal the identity of the nasent child appeared in the local newspaper recently. It said, "Medical experts take issue with the term **'fetal heartbeat,'** and they say the heart is not developed enough to produce a heartbeat at six weeks." According to the American College of Obstetricians & Gynecologists, the "heartbeat" heard on ultrasound is the machine translating electronic impulses that signify fetal cardiac activity into a heartbeat-like sound. This is ultimately the source of the comment that the politician made (and cited earlier) that the heartbeat observed by ultrasound is a "fake" sound[1] (see p. xi). Ultrasound is the transmission of sound waves into the body with a transducer which also "listens to" the echoes of those sounds. The sounds when they're up against a heartbeat will beat rhythmically as the heartbeat would be rhythmic. If a fetal heartbeat is observed, then there is a heartbeat present. The above is a direct color video of an image of a four-chamber heart at about 30 days post conception showing a heartbeat at 120 BPM, which is quite a bit faster than a maternal heartbeat which averages only about 72 BPM. Thus, two separate heartbeats are present. **(See www.womenlifechoice.com).**

1. Ashford M: Physicians speak out against bill. Omaha World-Herald, p. A3, Jan. 23, 2023.

FIGURE 4-13

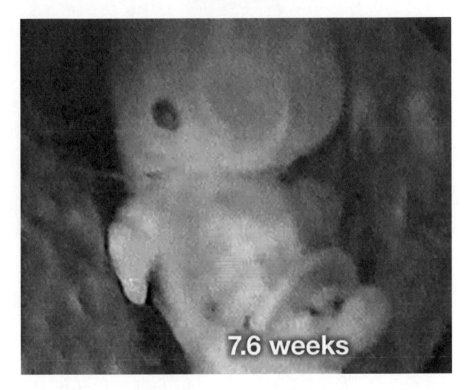

7.6 weeks

**7.6 WEEKS GESTATIONAL AGE
(5.6 WEEKS FETAL AGE)**

Figure 4-13: The nascent child at 7.6 weeks gestational age and 5.6 weeks fetal age by direct color photography. The arms and legs can now be seen; the large reddish area in the mid-torso is the heart, which is already beating at a separate rate from its mother at this age. (Photo: Thomas W. Hilgers, MD).

Also, the frontal lobes of the brain can be seen and electrical brain waves at this stage have been recorded, but the brain requires 25–27 for its functional capacity to become complete.

FIGURE 4-14

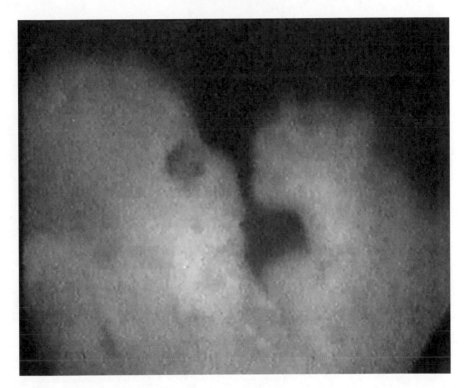

8.1 WEEKS

Figure 4-14: Profile of fetus at 8.1 weeks gestational age, 6.1 weeks fetal age. The right eye, right hand, the profile with the nose and lips visible are shown. The right hand is moving closer to the child's mouth in what appears to be an attempt to suck its thumb or hand. (Photo: Thomas W. Hilgers, MD.)

FIGURES 4-15A AND 4-15B

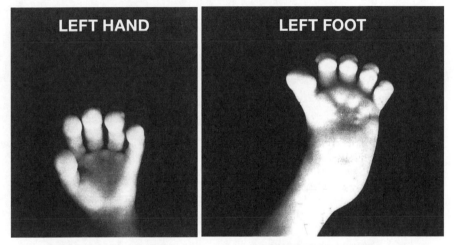

LEFT HAND
LEFT FOOT

FIGURE 4-15A   **FIGURE 4-15B**

Figures 4-15A and 4-15B: The fingers and thumb of the left hand (4-15A) and left foot (4-15B) at the beginning of the eighth to ninth week gestational age (sixth to seventh week fetal age). **Fingerprints** are forming. Large and small toes of the left foot at the beginning of the seventh week (fetal age) (4-15B).

FIGURES 4-16A, 16B, AND 16C

4-16A   **4-16B**   **4-16C**

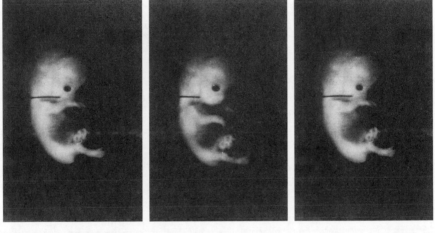

Figure 4-16A–C: Davenport Hooker's work showing movement at 8.5 weeks gestational age and 6.5 weeks fetal age. A horsehair is used to stroke and stimulate the right cheek of the embryo in Figure 4-16A, the right arm drops down in Figure 4-16B and returns to near its starting position in Figure 4-16C. This was first published in 1939.

FIGURES 4-17A–C

4-17A   4-17B   4-17C

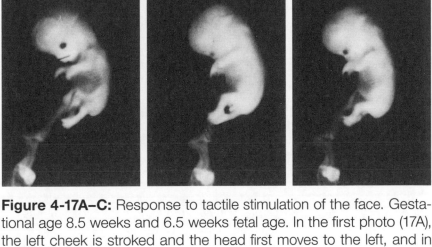

Figure 4-17A–C: Response to tactile stimulation of the face. Gestational age 8.5 weeks and 6.5 weeks fetal age. In the first photo (17A), the left cheek is stroked and the head first moves to the left, and in Figure 17B moves back to the right. In Figure 17C, the nascent child moves back to near the starting position.

[From: Actual motion pictures taken by Davenport Hooker, PhD, published 1939.]

FIGURE 4-18

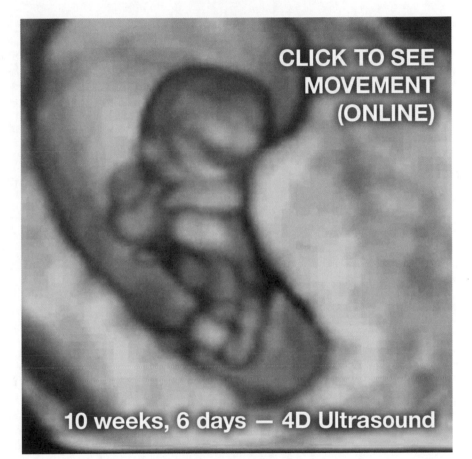

10 WEEKS, 6 DAYS

Figure 4-18: A 3- and 4-dimensional ultrasound of the nascent child at 10 weeks 6 days gestational age (8 weeks 6 days fetal age) (Saint Paul VI Institute Reproductive ultrasound Center). A 4-D ultrasound of the same baby with its extraordinary level of movement is included in the free video (www.womanlifechoice.com).

FIGURE 4-19

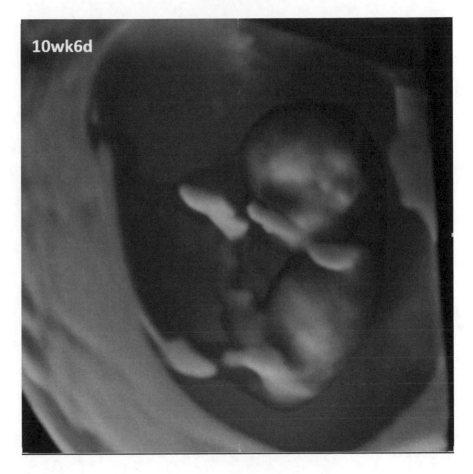

10 WEEKS, 6 DAYS

Figure 4-19: 3-dimensional ultrasound of the nascent child at gestational age of 10 weeks 6 days and 8 weeks, 6 days fetal age (Saint Paul VI Institute Reproductive ultrasound Center). An ultrasound smoothing technology has been used to produce an even more realistic picture. This child is within the first trimester of pregnancy when most abortions are performed.

FIGURE 4-20A–C

11 WEEKS
RESPONSE TO EXTERNAL STIMULATION

| 4-20A | 4-20B | 4-20C |

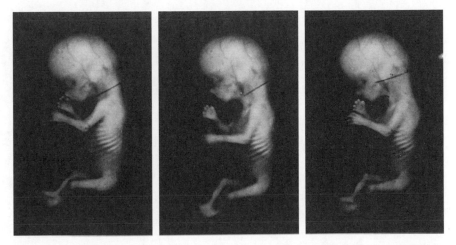

Figure 4-20A–C: Nascent child at a gestational age of 11 weeks (9 weeks fetal age) responding to tactile stimulation of the face with a hair. Backward movement of both arms in response to stimulation. Caudal movement of both forearms and hands more pronounced on the ipsilateral than on the contralateral side but without extension of the elbow. Return to normal fetal posture of the upper extremities (Figure 20C). The time between frames 20A and 20B is 0.125 seconds and between 20B and 20C is 1.06 seconds. (From: Hooker D: A Preliminary Atlas of Early Human Fetal Activity. From: The Ladd Laboratory of the Department of Anatomy, University of Pittsburgh School of Medicine. Published by the author, Davenport Hooker, PhD, p. 34 — Plate No. 26, 1939).

FIGURE 4-21
FROM HUNTER, 1774

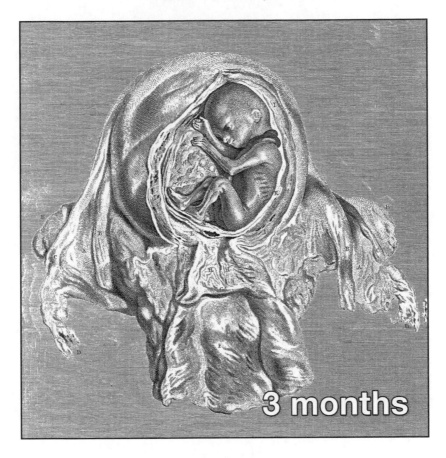

3 MONTHS
HUNTER: 1774

FIGURE 4-22

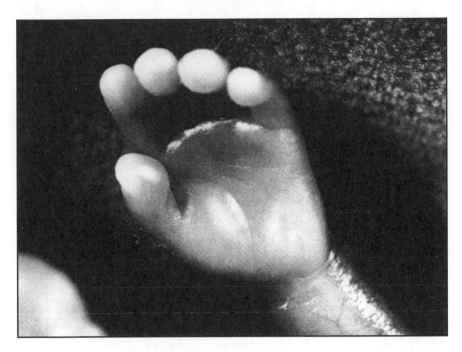

LEFT HAND AT 14 WEEKS OF AGE.

The author had a nascent child that was spontaneously miscarried. While the author was holding this child, there were attempts by the child to breathe. In addition, the child exhibited a Moro (startle) reflex, usually thought of as being present only in newborn, full-term babies.

FIGURE 4-23

3D ULTRASOUND AT 16 WEEKS, 6 DAYS, APPEARS TO BE SMILING

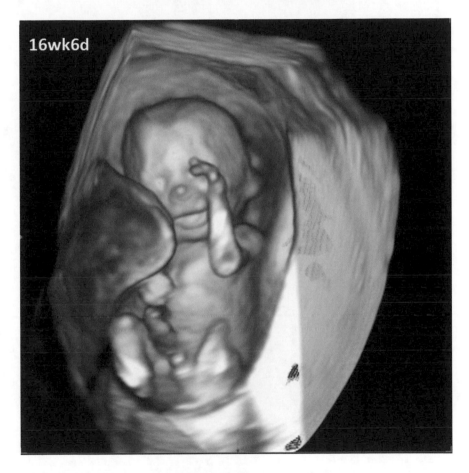

**16 WEEKS, 6 DAYS
GESTATIONAL AGE
(14 WEEKS, 6 DAYS FETAL AGE)**

FIGURE 4-24

3D ULTRASOUND AT 16 WEEKS, 6 DAYS GESTATIONAL AGE. SAME VIEW AS IN FIG. 4-23 WITH ADDITION OF "SMOOTHING" TECHNOLOGY AVAILABLE ON ULTRASOUND.

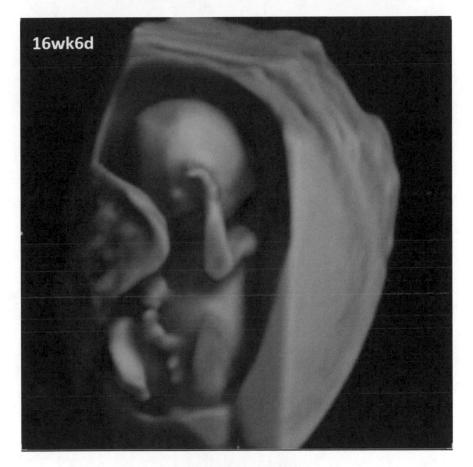

16wk6d

**16 WEEKS, 6 DAYS
GESTATIONAL AGE
14 WEEKS, 6 DAYS
FETAL AGE
BABY BOY**

FIGURE 4-25

**MOUTH WIDE OPEN, 3D ULTRASOUND
AT 16 WEEKS GESTATIONAL AGE
14 WEEKS FETAL AGE**

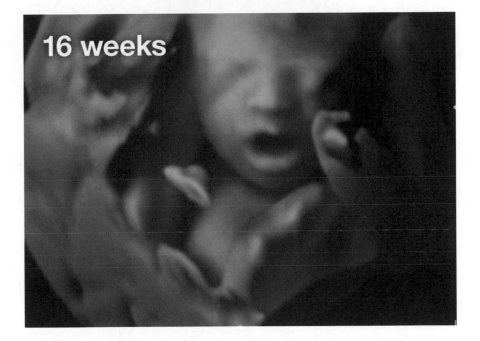

MOUTH WIDE OPEN

FIGURE 4-26

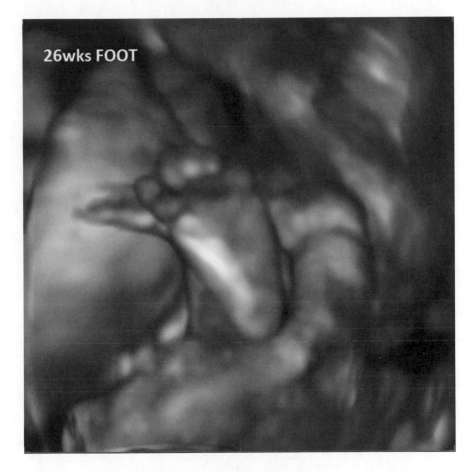

3D ULTRASOUND
LEFT FOOT AND TOES — 26 WEEKS
GESTATIONAL AGE
24 WEEKS FETAL AGE

FIGURE 4-27

**3D ULTRASOUND AT 26 WEEKS,
RIGHT HAND ON THE BROW**

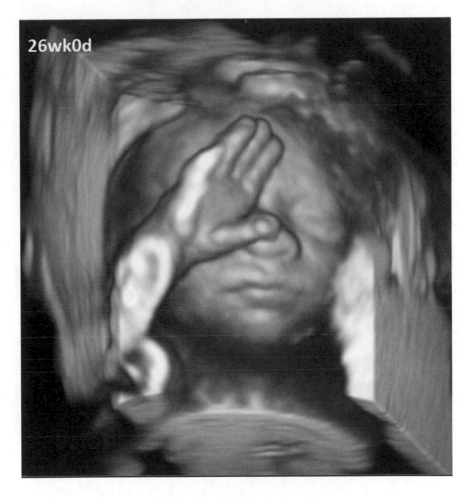

**26 WEEKS
GESTATIONAL AGE
(24 WEEKS FETAL AGE)**

FIGURE 4-28

**3D ULTRASOUND AT 26 WEEKS
WITH MOUTH WIDE OPEN**

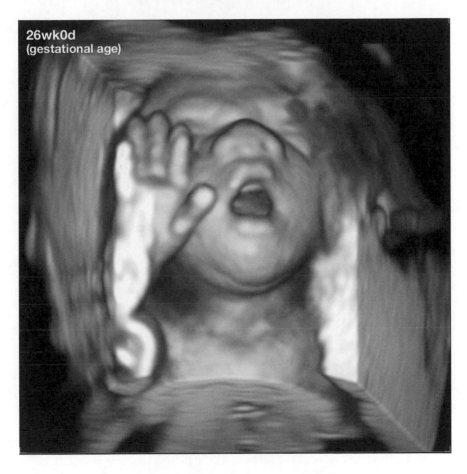

26wk0d
(gestational age)

**MOUTH OPEN — 26 WEEKS
GESTATIONAL AGE**

(24 WEEKS FETAL AGE)

FIGURE 4-29

3D ULTRASOUND OF FACIAL FEATURES AT 26 WEEKS (USING "SMOOTHING" TECHNIQUES AVAILABLE ON 3D ULTRASOUND). FROM SAINT PAUL VI INSTITUTE REPRODUCTIVE ULTRASOUND CENTER.

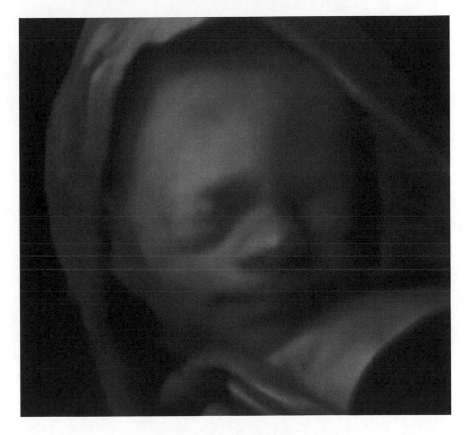

26 WEEKS GESTATIONAL AGE (24 WEEKS FETAL AGE)

FIGURE 4-30

FROM HUNTER, 1774 AT 6 MONTHS

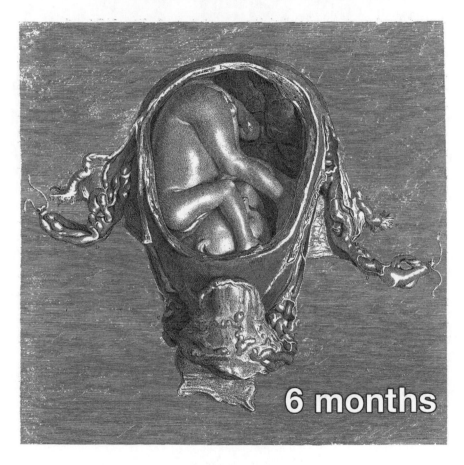

6 MONTHS
HUNTER, 1774

FIGURE 4-31

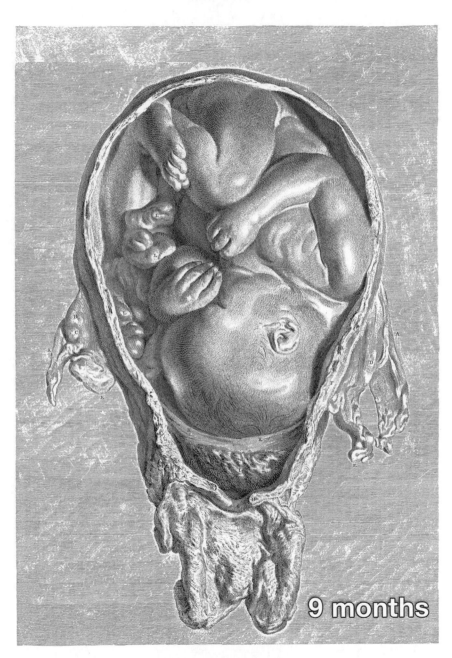

9 MONTHS
HUNTER: 1774

FIGURE 4-32

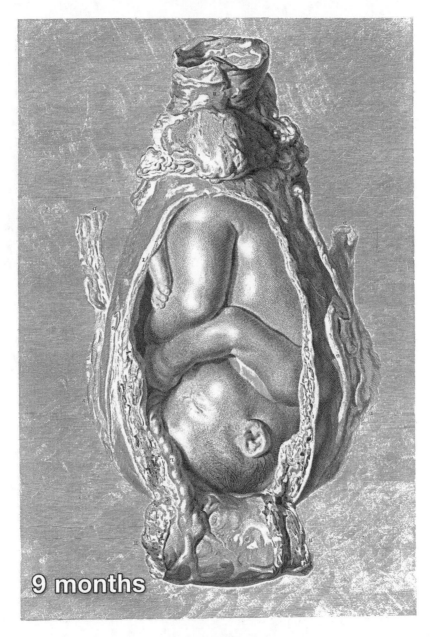

9 MONTHS
HUNTER 1774

FIGURE 4-33

3D ULTRASOUND AT 38 WEEKS, SUCKING THE THUMB[1]

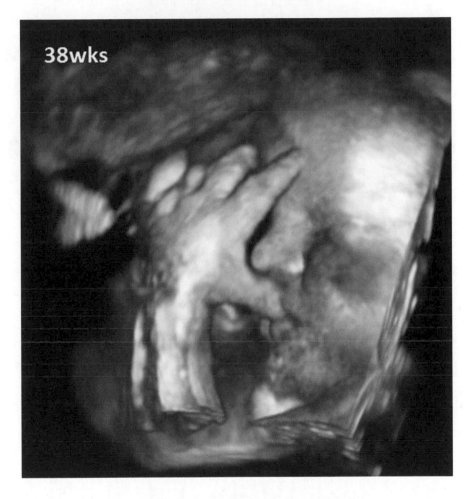

38 WEEKS — SUCKING THUMB
36 WEEKS FETAL AGE

Thumb sucking has been observed much earlier than this — early attempts have been seen in the first trimester of pregnancy.

A SET OF TWINS

FIGURE 4-34

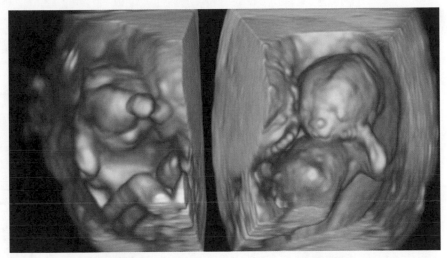

TWIN A   **TWIN B**

FIGURE 4-35

3D ULTRASOUNDS
AT 11, 19, 27, AND 37 WEEKS
THE *IN UTERO* CONNECTIONS OF THE *IN UTERO*
SPECTRUM OF HUMAN EXISTENCE

11 Weeks   **19 Weeks**

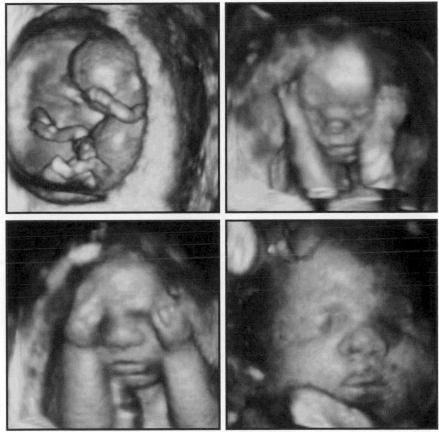

 27 Weeks   **37 Weeks**

FIGURE 4-36[1]

THE LIFELONG SPECTRUM OF THE HUMAN LIFE CONNECTION: THE GROWTH AND LIFELONG MATURATION OF THE MALE HUMAN PERSON FROM CONCEPTION THROUGH ITS NATURAL END

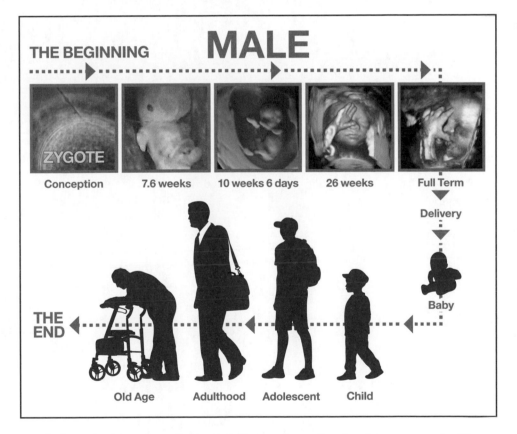

1. At each stage along the human life spectrum, the visual appearance is different. This is part of the human development process from conception (the zygote) through the end of life.

FIGURE 4-37[1]

THE LIFELONG SPECTRUM OF THE HUMAN LIFE CONNECTION: THE GROWTH AND LIFELONG MATURATION OF THE FEMALE HUMAN PERSON FROM CONCEPTION THROUGH ITS NATURAL END

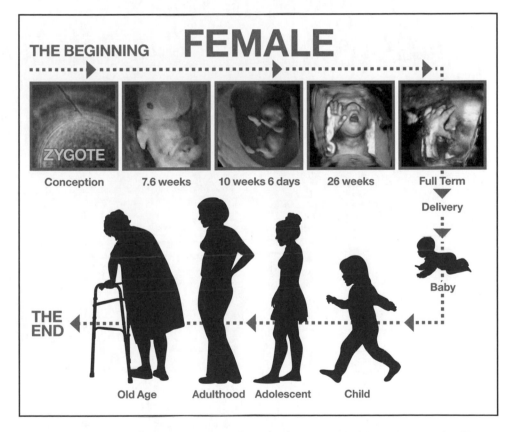

1. At each stage along the human life spectrum, the visual appearance is different. This is part of the human development process from conception (the zygote) through the end of life.

Chapter 5

The Quiz!

Place the name of the subject in the photograph for each of the following photos.

See if you can match up with
a group of 5 year olds.

THESE NEXT PHOTOS SHOW
COMPARATIVE ANATOMY

FIGURE 5-1:

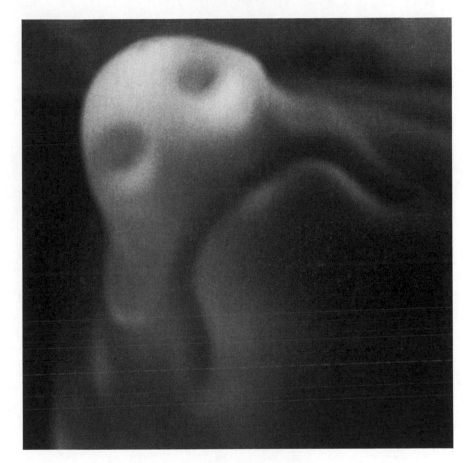

WHAT IS THIS SUBJECT?

1. _____

* Pictures 1, 2, 3A, B and C 4 and 5 From: Miller K.: What Does it Mean to be One of Us. LIFE Magazine, November 1996.

Answers on page 102.

FIGURE 5-2:

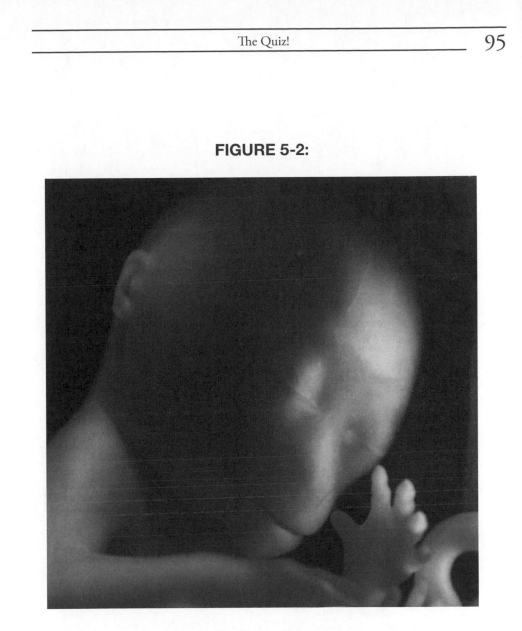

WHAT IS THIS SUBJECT?

2. _____

*The bluish discoloration over the left eye was in the original photo

FIGURE 5-3A-C:

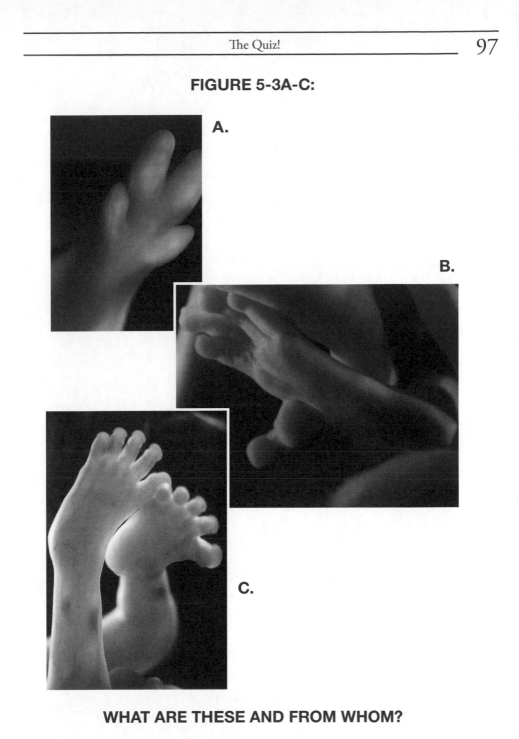

A.

B.

C.

WHAT ARE THESE AND FROM WHOM?

3A. _____

3B. _____

3C. _____

**THIS IS A PREGNANCY-RELATED
ULTRASOUND PHOTOGRAPH**

FIGURE 5-4:

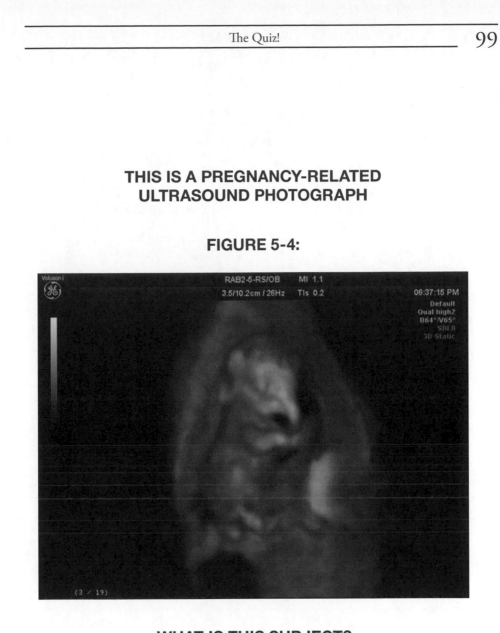

WHAT IS THIS SUBJECT?

5-4: _____

FIGURE 5-5:

MAN'S HAND

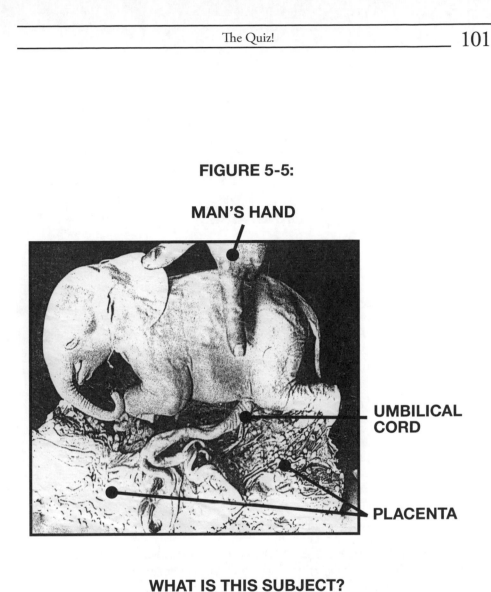

UMBILICAL CORD

PLACENTA

WHAT IS THIS SUBJECT?
(USE THE MAN'S HAND TO ESTIMATE SIZE)

5-5: _____

** Picture 4 from personal communication: regarding early intrauterine life with a placenta and the elephant.

ANSWERS:

Figure 5-1: **Pig**

Figure 5-2: **Monkey**

Figure 5-3 A-C   3A: **Pig's Hoof**

3B: **Monkey's Foot**

3C: **Human foot**

Figure 5-4: **Ultrasound photograph of an elephant in utero in its early stages of development**

Figure 5-5: **An elephant at early stages after being miscarried**

Special note: There is a science called comparative anatomy, and with an understanding of this science, an early development can be positively identified by examining the embryological anatomy.

Chapter 6

For Mature Eyes Only

The photographs in this section are **horrifying**! They represent the **violence, ugliness** and **dismemberment** that is human abortion. They may be difficult for some who view them, but as a culture, **we must know!** It is recommended that **parental guidance be implemented** for children who are at least **12 years or younger**.

FIGURE 6-1

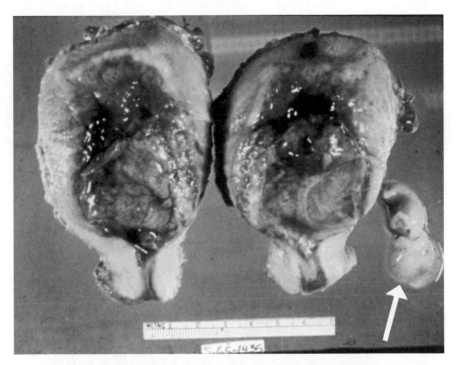

6 WEEK ABORTION BY HYSTERECTOMY

The nascent child is at the arrow (intact with the head down at the arrow).

FIGURE 6-2

6 WEEKS SUCTION ABORTION

The left shoulder girdle, arm, forearm, and hand are highlighted. This photograph shows a very horrific **dismemberment** (by suction) of this nascent child.

FIGURE 6-3

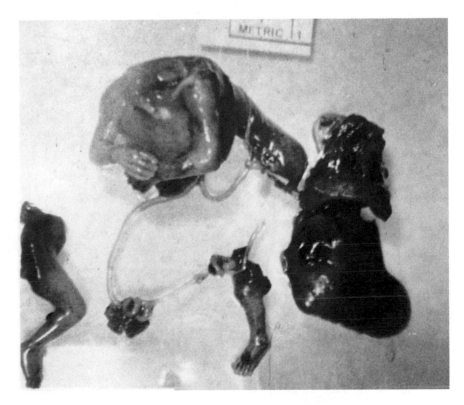

8 WEEKS D&C ABORTION

The photograph shows a very horrific **dismemberment**
(by D&C) of this nascent human child.

FIGURE 6-4

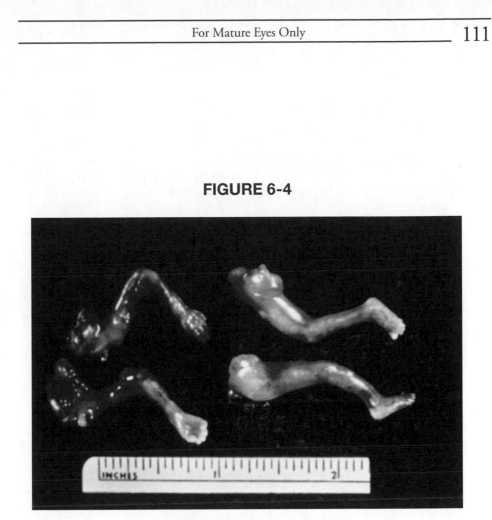

9 WEEKS D&C ABORTION

Abortion carried out by dilation (of the cervix) and curettage
(D&C) resulting in **gross dismemberment**.

FIGURE 6-5

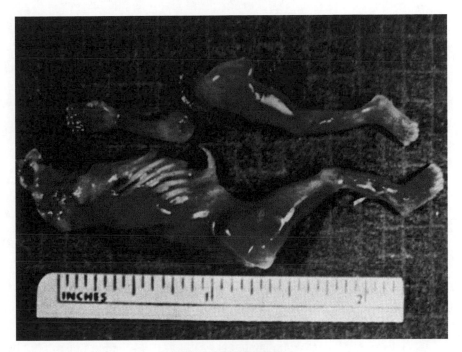

**D&E ABORTION
(DISMEMBERMENT)
12 WEEKS**

FIGURE 6-6

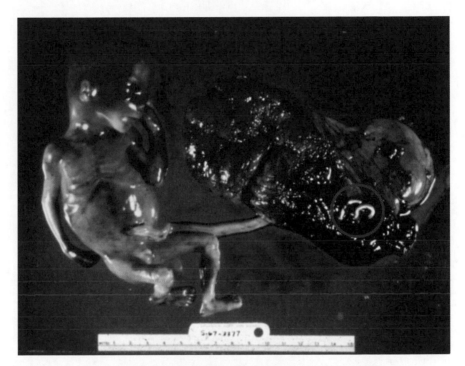

IV PITOCIN¹ ABORTION AT 14 WEEKS
IUD* IN PLACENTA
(circled in red)

*IUD = Intrauterine device

1. Pitocin is a medication used to stimulate uterine contractions, and at times it is used to produce abortion.

FIGURE 6-7

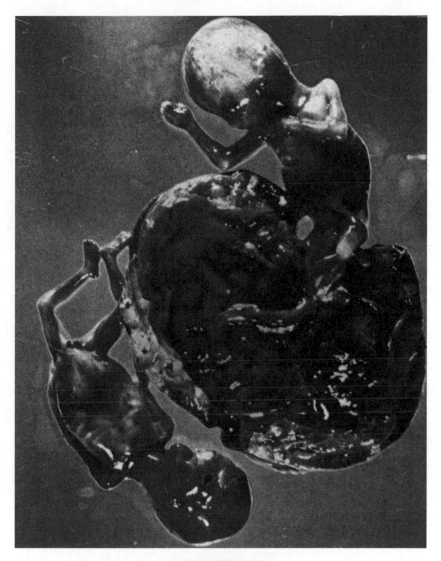

**14 WEEKS
TWIN ABORTION
BY WAY OF INSTILLATION OF 20% SALINE
(SALT SOLUTION) INDUCTION OF LABOR**

**THE RED DISCOLORATION IS CAUSED BY THE
20% SALINE SOLUTION (HYPERTONIC SALINE)
WHICH BURNS THE FRAGILE SKIN OF THE CHILD**

FIGURE 6-8

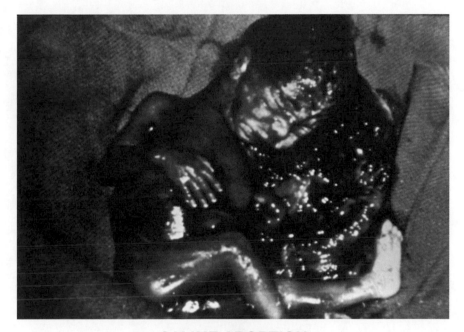

SALINE ABORTION
19 WEEKS

The red color of the skin is due to the skin being
burned by the 20% saline (salt solution).

FIGURE 6-9
PARTIAL BIRTH ABORTION

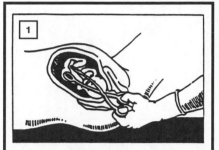

1. Guided by ultrasound, the abortionist grabs the baby's leg with forceps.

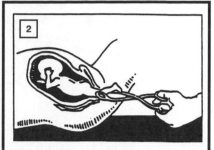

2. The abortionist delivers the baby's entire body, except for the head.

3. The baby's leg is pulled out into the birth canal.

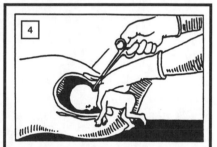

4. The abortionist jams scissors into the baby's skull. The scissors are then opened to enlarge the hole.

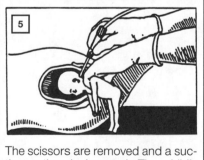

5. The scissors are removed and a suction cather is inserted. The child's brains are sucked out, causing the skull to collapse. The dead baby is then removed.

From: Susan B. Anthony List, P.O. Box 98008, Washington DC 20090-8008

FIGURE 6-10

COLLAPSED SKULL (AT THE RED ARROWS) FROM THE SUCTION CATHETER INSERTED INTO THE HEAD TO SUCTION IT OUT TO FACILITATE THE DEATH AND COLLAPSE THE SKULL TO FACILITATE ITS DELIVERY (PARTIAL BIRTH ABORTION)

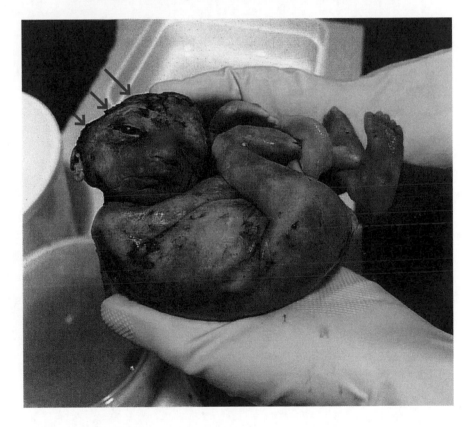

1. From: Dorman S: Aborted Babies Discovered in DC may indicate Infanticide after attempted abortions, Live Action News, April 1, 2022.

FIGURE 6-11

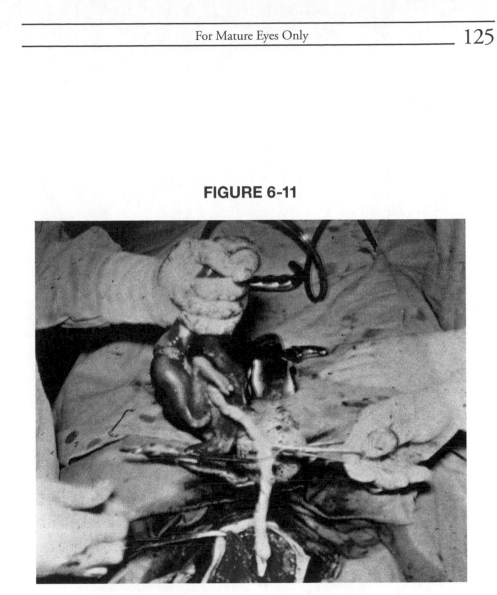

Hysterotomy (like a c-section) at 24 weeks

FIGURE 6-12

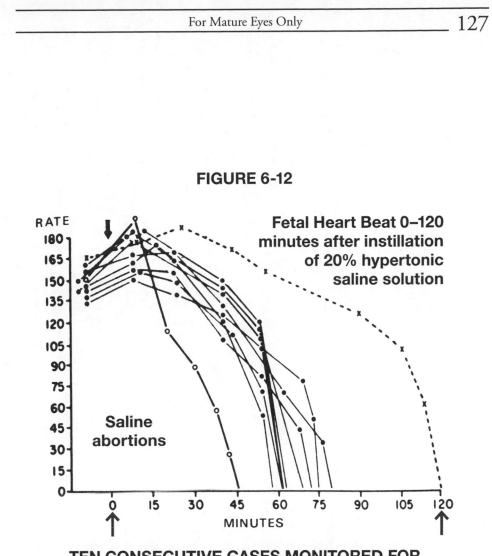

Fetal Heart Beat 0–120 minutes after instillation of 20% hypertonic saline solution

Saline abortions

TEN CONSECUTIVE CASES MONITORED FOR FETAL HEART RATE AFTER AMNIOINFUSION OF HYPERTONIC SALINE.

IT REVEALS THE DECREASE IN THE FETAL HEARTBEAT TO ZERO AS THE CHILD IS DYING!

1. Kerenyi TD: Outpatient Intra-amniotic Injection of Hypertonic Saline. Clinical Obstet Gynec 14: 137, 1971

FIGURE 6-13

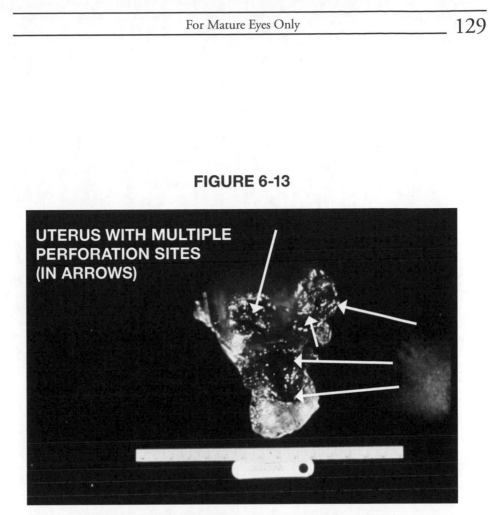

UTERUS WITH MULTIPLE PERFORATION SITES (IN ARROWS)

PERFORATIONS OF THE UTERUS WITH FIRST TRIMESTER ABORTION

This picture is an example of a uterus removed (hysterectomy) in a teenage girl because of multiple perforations and uncontrolled hemorrhage from a first trimester abortion.

• STOLEN IDENTITY •

FIRST, JIM CROW LAWS:
NOW, BABY-X LAWS

His eyes do not see
Her skin does not feel
Their brain does not recall
She can move and her limbs can also
He cannot walk, he cannot lift
But their brain does not recall

She has very little hair, no curls to see
They are not educated, but eventually can be
She can eventually love, but not now
They do not hate and do not cry
But their brain does not recall, it is at the beginning
        of a 25–27 year development path

But now **the knife enters their space**
They are **innocent** of all crimes
The knife **tears each apart** with equal vengeance
Is this **equity**? A **new form perhaps**?
Jim Crow hated and then destroyed many generations
Baby-X hate is now the target

It **cannot be love** when it is so **vicious, ugly** and **lethal**
Baby-X laws are the new Jim Crow laws
They both derive from previous hate and hurt
The outcomes are similar, nearly identical and usually final

First Jim Crow: Now Baby-X
The true identity of Baby-X continues to be stolen
Shame on the adults that feel no pain
But these same adults have their own pain, for which they deny!
But please God be with them all on this Day!

Thomas W. Hilgers, MD

Co-Founder
Saint Paul VI Institute for the Study
of Human Reproduction

"Baby-X" equals a human baby in its mother's womb who is alive and has a developing brain, which is not fully developed until about age 25–27 years.

Chapter 7

Fifty Years of Near Universal Disinformation, Deception and Distortion

Of all of the issues that get a good deal of political coverage in the United States, there is no topic with more **disinformation, deception** and/or **distortion** than **the abortion issue**. This has been a consistent finding from even before *Roe v. Wade*, in response to the lead-up to the Supreme Court's 1973 decision and has continued to the present day. This chapter is intended to present some challenges to this **disinformation, deception** and **distortion** in an attempt to raise the level of awareness. I will list these in the following order:

1. **Medical terminology** is often used to describe the "embryo" and/ or the "fetus" to a group of people who are otherwise lay people. While these are relatively commonly used medical terms, it is also true that most people could probably not define what an embryo or

a fetus is. Furthermore, it is almost never stated that **human life is a spectrum of events** starting with the human zygote (the moment of conception) and progressing all the way through the pregnancy, to birth, infancy, childhood, adolescence, the teenage years, early adulthood, late adulthood and old age concluding with natural death. **All through this "spectrum of life" the connectivity from the moment of conception until the conclusion of life by natural causes is uninterrupted. This is what defines human life or the entirety of human existence.** Said in a different way, the formation of the human zygote is what leads eventually to all the stages of growth and development of the nascent child during pregnancy or any of the other stages of human existence.

2. It is often said there were **5,000 to 10,000 women who died from illegal abortion** (sometimes referred to as **"coat-hanger abortion"**) per year in the U.S. However, those numbers are grossly in error by a factor of 100 to 200 times. There is **absolutely no evidence** this number of women (or even close to it) occurred on a yearly basis. The only admission was **its fabrication!** In 1972, the year prior to the January 22, 1973 date of *Roe v. Wade*, there were 48 estimated maternal deaths from **both spontaneous and induced abortion, legal or not, reported by the National Center for Vital Statistics of the United States.** These data, which have been in existence for many years, show nowhere near the 5,000 to 10,000 maternal deaths per year occurring; it is extremely unlikely, if not impossible, for that number of maternal deaths to have been missed.

3. **Planned Parenthood** says adolescents **"are going to have 'sex' no matter what we do or say!"** However, it is well known that 50-60% of teenagers do **not** have sexual intercourse and the real story, which has gone almost completely uninvestigated, is how is it, in what otherwise is a hyper-erotic culture, that this fairly large percentage of young people in their teen years do **not** have sexual encounters. This is something requiring a lot more study and, while we do know it has to do with prevailing values within the family culture (see appendix), this may actually be at the heart of a positive solution to this issue.

4. In the March 2017 issue of *Fertility & Sterility* (the major journal of the American Society of Reproductive Medicine), a letter submitted by a doctor who performs *in vitro* fertilization (test-tube babies) was entitled, "The Unscientific Nature of the Concept that 'Human Life Begins at Fertilization' and Why it Matters." This is a striking commentary by a person who, in his own work, has shown decisively that life begins at fertilization (a formation of the human zygote often referred to as the time of conception). This author has never seen a pregnancy in his clinic that did not begin with a human zygote. While he is a "**fertilization denier** (or a **conception denier**, or a **zygote denier** or a **human life denier**)," this is blatantly false, but was re-published by a major medical journal in the United States with world-wide distribution in the field of human reproduction. It also points out **the corruption occurring within medicine** and the political nature of this topic existing within the medical profession.

5. Abortion is often spoken of as a part of "**women's health**" or "**reproductive healthcare**." However, **an abortion is not a part of health**, it is a part of a **lethal expression of the capability of the doctor to terminate life**. Such termination has been rampant in the United States across many generations and some falsely insist that it is, in some manner, a part of "women's health," "reproductive healthcare" or, generically, "healthy for women."

6. As you see demonstrations on the news, you often see a sign reading, "**My body … my choice**." However, in a woman who is pregnant — even at the earliest stages of pregnancy — the baby is a completely separate entity relying upon the love, care and respect the mother has for her nascent child. This child is **not a part of her "body."** The **blood types are often different**, the **heart rate is different from the mother's** and **the immune system** is different. **The DNA types are different too!** Furthermore, these babies have a genetic linkage to their mothers. While it is true women can make choices (often spoken of as "**pro-choice**"), the choices available to them are the ones occurring **before** they get pregnant. **The choice to lethalize their nascent child is not hers, nor is it ethically her doctor's.** *First do no harm!* The **choices she has available**

to her should be responsible and accepting and related to the love, care and respect the mother gives to her new child.

7. **"I have a right to an abortion!"** This is not an uncommon statement also stated by women who might be carrying a placard at the time of a pro-abortion rally. However, **the right to abortion does not exist,** it is manufactured! It does not exist in any religion in the world, nor in any specific documents related to the governance in the United States of America. In the sense of claiming a "right to abortion" there is a religious fervor existing and abortion is seen as part of that religion. The United States Constitution, in its First Amendment says the government shall not install or establish a formal religion, so there are definitely legitimate reasons to consider and call this "right" to abortion, an area where with state-sponsored props to continue that religion would be a violation of the First Amendment.

8. Senator Lindsey Graham suggested **the cut-off for abortion should be at 15 weeks, which means if the woman is 15 weeks or less, an abortion should be legal.** He uses as a justification to this a previous vote in the United States Senate which set 15 weeks as some type of a magic marker. However, more than 90% of all abortions in the United States are performed at 15 weeks or earlier, so this recommendation makes virtually no major impact on the move towards reducing the number of abortions in the United States. However, this fact has been kept from the American people.

9. **Abortion is an emotional issue!** It is true that abortion produces a good deal of emotional reaction whether you have had an abortion, are contemplating abortion, or are opposed to abortion; the emotion exists. The question many years ago should have been asked, **"Are our emotions trying to tell us something?"** The answer is *"yes, they are!"* And, while there are multiple components to an abortion decision telling a woman this is her "only option," the last portion of the decision making is the catastrophic annihilation of her own baby, a decision she will need to live with for the rest of her life. This causes **emotional pain** as well and is more difficult to eliminate. But that pain has been justified because only a certain

percentage of women say they have such emotional reactions. As an obstetrician with more than 40 years of experience, I can tell you that whenever I take a medical history from a woman who has had an induced abortion, it is almost universal, even though many years have passed, for an emotional reaction to occur. **Rationalization can be defined as the use of what appears to be good reasons in the place of real reasons.**

10. The term **universal healthcare for women** is often used as well. Planned Parenthood utilizes this approach, and Planned Parenthood does not provide universal healthcare to women and does not even come close to it. What they do provide is very limited care, care limited to contraception and abortion. In some cases, Pap smears may be performed or a referral to a local doctor may be made, but Planned Parenthood does not provide the care; and yet their services are supported with more than $500 million per year in financial support from the federal treasury in addition to large numbers of major donors. If the people who provide abortions really cared for the women they are performing the abortions on, they would provide their services at no charge.

11. Politicians have said abortion is okay if it is **safe, legal and rare**. This is the famous quote President Bill Clinton used in his campaign for the presidency. **The major part of this, which is not accurate, is the term, "rare."** After Clinton became President, the number of abortions performed in the United States, whether it be by surgical abortion or medical abortion did not change much at all. But **because he said he would promise for it to be "rare," people believed him**. It is just another lie that the pro-abortion lobby has spewed.

12. It is said that contraception prevents abortion. While there are some studies suggesting that is the case, a major study showing the use of technological forms of contraception on the same graph as the increase in the number of abortions performed, strongly suggests contraception increases the abortion rate (see appendix). In addition, the author has heard speakers from Planned Parenthood admit their contraception programs are vital to their very effort

to promote abortion because abortion is a big money-maker for Planned Parenthood, and contraception increases the number of women who become pregnant and then "need an abortion."

13. It has been said that there were more than 1 million illegal abortions per year in the United States before *Roe v. Wade*; however, that is not nearly so much the truth as one might imagine. Even Planned Parenthood suggested the "1 million" total came from poorly devised data. The only place in the United States where any type of data were generated was out of New York City and that was then extrapolated to the whole of the United States. I trained in obstetrics and gynecology in the pre-*Roe* era, and in all the years I have practiced obstetrics and gynecology but also those years when I was in training before *Roe*, I only saw one patient who had an attempted illegal abortion. **In that case, we were able to treat the sepsis and, not only save the mother, but also save the baby.**

ABORTION ALTERNATIVES

What about alternatives to abortion? In many books I have written on the abortion issue, I have focused a lot on the question of **alternatives to abortion.** However, the only alternative that is presented is always contraception. The emergency pregnancy service groups staffed and operated by individuals who are pro-life, have been literally attacked since the recent Supreme Court decision *Dobbs v. Jackson*. This tells us a couple of things. First of all, it shows **the people who are pro-abortion have really no concern about putting together programs to help the women who are pregnant and in distress**. These pro-life programs and facilities have been attacked in vicious ways and all too frequently torched. **Incidentally, the pro-life pregnancy services receive no federal funds, whereas Planned Parenthood gets it all.** This is a reflection of **the government's anti-religious view** since these are staffed by people who are usually people of faith. In so doing, the government denies the "faith" the personnel of Planned Parenthood need to exhibit in order to be "good" contraceptive and abortion counselors. Eventually, to correct this problem in favor of life, this dichotomy in opposite directions needs to be resolved or dealt with in, at least, an equal fashion. At this time the approach is completely one-sided and is thus highly discriminatory.

There has been a near universal condition which accompanies almost all women who seek and adopt abortion (see Figure 7-1). This could be referred to as *"social abortion."* It can be defined as **a rejection of a pregnant woman by those close to her,** such as a **boyfriend, husband, friends, relatives, physicians,** etc. Is it also the **primary reality** and is due to **nascephobia and maternaphobia**. Most medical and surgical abortions are preceded by this rejection, **placing pressure on the woman to abort the pregnancy due to a lack of support. The pressure is led by the cold approach of the abortion lobby! Suppress and reject.**

FIGURE 7-1

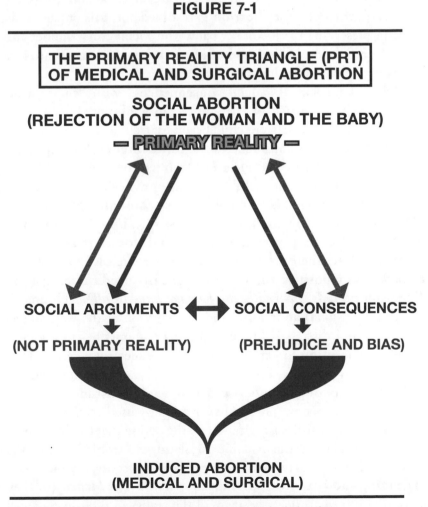

THE PRIMARY REALITY TRIANGLE (PRT)
OF MEDICAL AND SURGICAL ABORTION

SOCIAL ABORTION
(REJECTION OF THE WOMAN AND THE BABY)
— PRIMARY REALITY —

SOCIAL ARGUMENTS ⟷ SOCIAL CONSEQUENCES

(NOT PRIMARY REALITY)   (PREJUDICE AND BIAS)

INDUCED ABORTION
(MEDICAL AND SURGICAL)

The Primary Reality Triangle of medical and surgical abortion.

Ultimately, we accept **"social abortion,"** the rejection of the woman who is pregnant and distressed **by submitting her to a vicious and violent solution to her "social consequences."** This is accomplished through various **social arguments** which are **not** the primary reality. **The rejection that occurs is the primary reality**, and it is the great obstacle to finding positive solutions for women who are pregnant and distressed. **There are solutions to "social abortion"** which can be described in general as **positive alternatives to abortion.** It looks at the reality of the rejection that has been placed upon the woman who is pregnant (sometimes that rejection is placed upon the woman by her own initiative). **Once the rejection that is "social abortion" is resolved, the need for abortion is resolved** and this enhances her life while preserving the life of her baby. **The social consequences are often the reflection of prejudice, bias and antagonism. That is the underbelly of the rejections!**

The juxtaposition of **"social consequences"** with **"social arguments"** has become one of the most commonly cited reasons for abortion. Basically the nascent child becomes irrelevant in this view but **this rationale is weak** and reflects **the unwillingness to respond** in a positive way to these consequences. Of course, once abortion is legal and available **"on demand,"** the **"easy way out"** becomes the solution. **What has been missed is how few of these consequences are really solved and how many are harmed by a surgical/medical approach that is aimed at emptying the uterus and does not address the social abortion.** There are better solutions that are easy to bypass **for the lack of any positive energy to become involved in being a part of the solution.** *Is this really the best we have to offer?* Ultimately, by accepting **"social abortion,"** and the rejection of the woman who is pregnant and distressed (**maternaphobia**) submits her to **a vicious and violent solution** to her **"social consequences"** as a result of various **social arguments. These, unfortunately, do not address the Primary Reality of pregnancy under these circumstances.**

For many years now, physicians have rightly used ultrasound to be able to assess fetal cardiac activity. While the notion that the "heartbeat" heard on ultrasound is the machine translating electronic impulses that signify fetal cardiac activity into a heartbeat-like sound, **is purposely misleading and is another attempt to *steal the true identity* of these nascent children** at the early stages of the reality of their lives. This is a relatively new insult to the preborn child. This technology has been used for over 50 years now in modem obstetrics and has never been thought of from a medical point of view to be "fake" or simply a sound generated arbitrarily by the ultrasound equipment. In fact, if we hear a heartbeat identified by ultrasound (which is widely used throughout all of medicine including by the physicians of the American College of Obstetricians & Gynecologists) **it does correctly reflect the true fetal heart beating.** These are the types of observations which continue to show up in the arguments on the abortion issue in ways meant to downgrade the reality of life, a new and unique life, which is present in the mother's womb, in this case designed to undercut the proposed heartbeat laws that are in many state legislatures. **Stolen identity is at work even in today's world and you don't have to go back 20 to 40 years to be able to identify it!** Incidentally, along that line, there are probably very few organizations (outside of Planned Parenthood) that are more **pro-abortion** than the American College of Obstetricians & Gynecologists. It clearly does not represent all doctors who take care of women who are pregnant, nor does it represent the nascent child.

WORDS COMMONLY USED

Viability: This is often defined as that stage of pregnancy after which the baby is capable of living outside the mother's womb. However, the term "viable" means "capable of living." The baby in the womb is also "capable of living" (and is actually living throughout the gestation) and can be classified as exhibiting *intracorporeal viability. Extracorporeal viability* should be considered a definition of viability existing if the baby has reached the age of being capable of surviving once born. The important point here is viability is often accepted as a moving target. That is to say, it will continue to be less and less in age and currently is 22 weeks, whereas at the time of *Roe v. Wade* it was 24-28 weeks.

"Keep your rosaries off of my ovaries": The ovaries are not the ones becoming pregnant. Rosaries, of course, are not ovaries. While this is a slang expression with the two words rhyming, they are grossly inaccurate. The accuracy of slang expressions designed to promote abortion should be double-checked with regard to their scientific accuracy. Such expressions take away the identity of the nascent child.

"A blob of protoplasm": This is a phrase used, especially early in the pro-abortion movement. It was another way in which to **dehumanize** the nascent human being and is completely out of step with what we now understand is a *spectrum of human life* defining a living human being from the moment of conception to the moment of natural death.

"This is a 'Catholic issue": This has its roots in a deeply biased view of religion. The view the Church is trying to convey to people is a teaching on abortion based in science and also scriptural statements such as "Whatever you do unto the least of my brethren, you do unto Me," (Mt 25:40–41). Even Catholics have been disarmed by this by joining those who favor abortion. Examples of this include Joe Biden, Nancy Pelosi, some bishops and cardinals, along with others. **The Church's position should not be quiet or intimidated!**

Chapter 8

The Future ... Protect, Protect and Protect!

There is perhaps no approach to the solution of a complex moral and social problem currently present than the **barbarism** with its **cruel tentacles** exhibited in state-approved abortion. It not only **destroys a new human life** at the beginning of its spectrum of life, it is a **brutal invasion** of a woman's body. In some ways, **it is more savage and brutal than forcible rape.** A sharp curette or a suction curette is thrust into the woman's body, going through the vagina, the cervical canal, and into the uterus, where the body of the nascent child is ground up, sliced into pieces, and removed from its life support. It should be **condemned by all people.** It is ultimately a question of developing a **pluralistic morality** on this issue. The Catholic Church's position will not be what is accepted as a national position on this issue nor was it accepted before *Roe.* That is not to say the Church will change its position — in fact I would hope it would not. At the same time, a provision needs to be encoded into law protecting people who have **conscientious objection**.

There have been politicians claiming "our democracy" is at stake because of "election deniers" or "climate deniers" in our electorate. Taking this approach protects them from being challenged on these issues when, in fact, they are not actually issues of conscience. This is not an approach to problem-solving belonging in a civilized society. In fact, it enforces a **much more important form of denial**; being a **"life denier"** when there is **far more scientific evidence on "life' than either the "elections" or "climate."**

In looking to the future, there are three words describing what needs to be done and what our plan of action should be:

PROTECT, PROTECT AND PROTECT!

First of all, **we must protect the right to live for those nascent children currently being destroyed** for no really good or ethically-balanced reason; the reasons are predominantly emotional — certainly this is not a reason balanced by the taking of that person's life. Keep in mind, these children are **completely innocent; they have not been provided due process** or an **appropriate trial. They are completely innocent! There is, in fact, no member of our society or our culture more innocent! The child in the womb has been viciously attacked in a brutal and inhumane way.**

As we begin to protect the right of this child to live — always the motivation of the pro-life movement — abortion is by itself not being "banned." While it is true some people classify this type of action as "banning abortion," **its main motivation has always been the protection of the very life of the preborn child who will be lost as a result of the abortion.** We must develop in our protection of the preborn child, a legitimate and intense ability to be consistent recognizing the saving of the child can be done in a way which enacts legal protections while at the same time recognizes most of this needs to be accomplished by **loving, caring and respecting the mother!**

By protecting the right to exist of the nascent child through legal means, an attitude or a values formation is developed — **a "respect for life"** if you will. **This is, indeed, the number one human rights issue of our day! Abortion is a crime against nature, against humanity, against God, against the community, against society and against**

the very future of our existence as a free society!

The **second part** of the **"Protect"** component is to not only **protect the mother, but also to provide supportive structures to her during the course of the pregnancy,** at the time of the delivery and then the time following. In this regard, **adoption** can and should be a realistic option and the stigma currently attached to the mother for putting a child up for adoption **needs to be abolished!** There are so many options for providing a more welcoming approach to the woman who is pregnant and distressed.

This involves developing programs for the woman who is pregnant and distressed along with the father who, in his own way, is also undergoing some level of distress, although it is of a different nature than for the mother. Both of these concerns need to be thought out clearly and developed. **Both the mother and the father need to be respected.** There is a **level of sexual retardation** involving the social attitude that puts sexual interaction **in the realm of "sexual recreation."** And yet, because procreation has been left out of the equation now for more than 60 years, a revolution in seeing social attitudes change to a more sincere, realistic and loving view of human sexuality is desperately needed!

This can all change with a better understanding of our human fertility and of our sexuality. **Understanding our fertility brings out respect for each other;** it abandons the "plumbing school of human sexuality." We should not look at the bedroom as the "center for the performing arts (or the back seat of a car, a park bench, etc.)." Unfortunately **the Playboy ethic established by Hugh Hefner distorted this view dramatically and Planned Parenthood became its enforcer and the government its main funding vehicle.**

But in knowing and understanding our fertility, we can develop S-P-I-C-E! This ultimately stands for a comprehensive view of our human sexuality and not to see each other, man and/or woman, as simply an object of sexual pleasure. The acronym **S-P-I-C-E** stands for: **Spiritual, Physical, Intellectual, Creative/Communicative,** and **Emotional/Psychological**. It is a multidimensional approach to human sexuality beginning to realize our sexuality is not all between our legs. In other words, **we must expand our sexual horizons.** When feminists say they know how their body works, the **actual reality is they do not know how their body works!** A great deal of progress has been made across the last 30 to 40 years with research predominantly undertaken at the **Saint Paul VI Institute for the Study of Human Reproduction**, to realize how sexuality can be expanded to the whole person as opposed to just portions of that individual or relationship. More about this can be obtained by looking up **Fertility*Care*™ Centers of America** (www.fertilitycare.org) and locating a teacher for the **CREIGHTON MODEL Fertility*Care*™ System** and the new women's health science of **NaProTECHNOLOGY®**. This provides an approach to family planning and women's health far beyond what is currently available in our culture. It actually **looks for the underlying causes of women's health issues** — specifically those women who are in the procreative age group. It teaches women and their spouses or boyfriends how to interact with each other in a way which expands their ability to see them as total people as opposed to just individuals relating to only one physical component. While our current culture focuses on how many different ways one can have physical sexual interaction, the concept of SPICE expands our sexual horizons to include the total dimensions of the human person. It establishes foundations upon which **long-term commitments in marriage can be made, the divorce rate can be decreased and how, in marriage, the relationship can be bonded.**

The third **"Protect"** is spelled out in **protecting our humanity by reinforcing the value of life.** As a nation, we were founded on the principles of "Life, Liberty and the Pursuit of Happiness." **One needs to consider whether or not liberty and the pursuit of happiness can in fact be accomplished when life is so disrespected and, for that matter, physically abolished.** I think we know from the last 50 to 60 years of this approach to problem solving — an approach which **encompasses the principle of lethalism — is a political process ultimately abandoning liberty and the pursuit of true happiness.**

Many years ago, when I was debating the main pro-abortion coordinator at the University of Minnesota, I mentioned the introduction of abortion into the culture will only lead to other lethal aspects. In fact, I have now lived long enough to see this reality. **Physician-assisted suicide** (the conjunction of these three words should never be seen in law or in print because a physician's role is not to produce death), has become a reality in a number of states particularly on the West Coast. This is **a form of euthanasia.** In the debate over parental rights in the

Virginia governor's race a couple of years ago, the governor, a pediatric specialist (which makes this even worse), said that if the baby is born with a congenital defect of some type, then he would sit down with the mother and decide what to do with the baby. One of the options, however, was to **euthanize the child after it is born. This is infanticide!** More recently, with late-term abortion, people have also used the term "infanticide." This is abortion performed until the moment of birth. Technically speaking, the term infanticide should belong to those who have been newly born, however, it seems legitimate to use the term infanticide in those babies who are so far along in their pregnancy as to be within a day or two of being born. This has also shown up with **Barack Obama's vote when in the Illinois legislature against medical care for babies born prematurely with abnormalities associated with it, and they should just be allowed to die.** This is reinforced in the most recent 2022 election by other politicians. **How more barbaric and cruel can one get?**

We cannot accept the notion that abortion, infanticide or euthanasia is "the best we have to offer!" In fact, it is so far from the best, anybody who wants America to become great again would automatically reject it. Those who do not want America to be great will pretty much automatically accept it. So, this becomes a distinguishing feature in those political races where one wants to find out if one is in favor or a **"culture of life"** or favors a **"culture of death."**

In the process of all of this, we have seen in the United States a crime wave which is itself barbaric and cruel. Homicide rates have increased, and gross hostility towards others has increased. The negative attitude towards changing these approaches shows us that we must not be afraid of excellence. It is rather the role of a Nazi-like mentality we need to fear. Those who said the election was about denying our democracy were actually the ones denying such democracy. **The level to which politicians lie and deceive and distort is overwhelming. We must be better than them!**

In medicine, there has developed a superior attitude that a group of experts in medicine suddenly become the final word in all of this. **It is a form of medical dictatorship** and doctors who are opposed to abortion, opposed to euthanasia, opposed to hostility towards others, are often facing antagonism, removal of their privileges, removal of their licenses, etc. It is indeed a hostility evolving because a group of medical doctors — often at the highest academic level — have developed a liberalism — a form of what is now called "progressivism" — and ultimately **a way they can control their environment, their colleagues and others.** It is in some ways new but is really a sign of **regressivism.** As I said earlier in this book, when I graduated medical school, it was still early in the change to a **dictatorship of relativism.** At our graduation, we recited the **Declaration of Geneva,** which was developed following and in response to the war crimes as part of the Nuremburg Trials in post-war Germany. It said, **"I will have the utmost respect for human life from the moment of conception."** (!!!) We must take a look back at the war crime trials, the original Declaration of Geneva which supported life and was even stronger than the Hippocratic Oath. We often in medicine say "First do no harm" and yet we have adopted the attitude that we should **"do harm** no matter what the cost!" **This latter ethic cannot and should not stand!**

Appendix

Abortion, its effect on the family, and other related data and graphs

APP-1

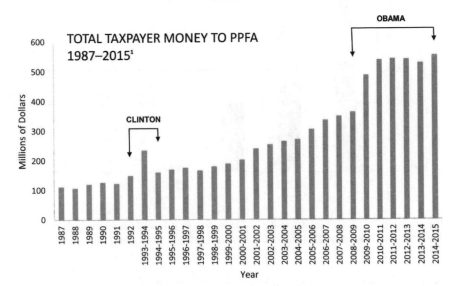

Figure App-1: The federal funding of Planned Parenthood from 1987 through 2014–2015. Citation: Gigant K: Your Tax Dollars at Work for Planned Parenthood. Celebrate Life. 25:42–45. PPFA Annual Report 2002, 2003, 2004, 2005, 2006, 2007, 2008, 2009, 2010, 2012, 2013, 2014.[1]

1. During these 28 years an estimated **10.2 billion dollars** was given to Planned Parenthood by the U.S. Government.

APP-2[1]

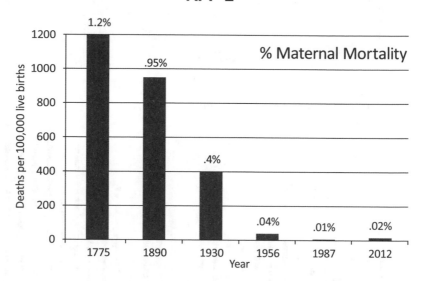

Figure App-2: Maternal Mortality in Deaths per 100,000 live Births. Data from the US only. Previous data may or may not be from the United States only (see below).

For data from 1987 to 2012: Center for Disease Control and Prevention. Pregnancy Mortality Surveillance System. U.S Department of Health and Human Services. January 21, 2016. http://www.cdc.gov/reproductivehealth/maternalinfanthealth/pmss.html

For data from 1775–1956: Gibbs RS: Impact of Infectious Diseases on Women's Health: 1776-2026, Obstet Gynecol 97:1019-1023, 2001. Gibbs RS does not specify whether data is from the US only. Their sources for these data are: Shorter E. A History of Women's Bodies. New York: Basic Books, 1982.

Bureau of the Census with the Cooperation of the Social Service Research Council. Historical statistics of the United States, colonial times to 1957. Washington DC: United States Government Printing Office, 1960.

Leavitt JW. Brought to bed. Childbearing in America, 1750-1950. New York: Oxford University Press, 1986.

1. From 1775 through 2012, there has been a decrease in maternal mortality by a factor of 60–120 times.

APP-3[1]

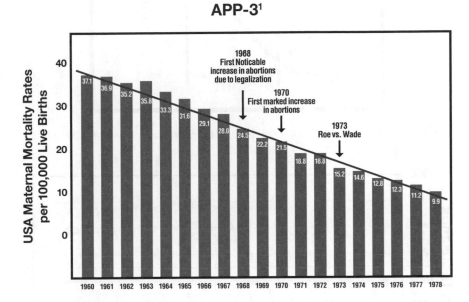

Figure App-3: Maternal Mortality Rates — USA 1960–1978 (From: Maternal Mortality Statistics, National Center for Health Statistics, 1960–1978)

1. From 1960 through 1978, there was **a steady decrease in the maternal mortality rate** in the United States unaffected by the introduction of legalized abortion.

APP-4 AND 5

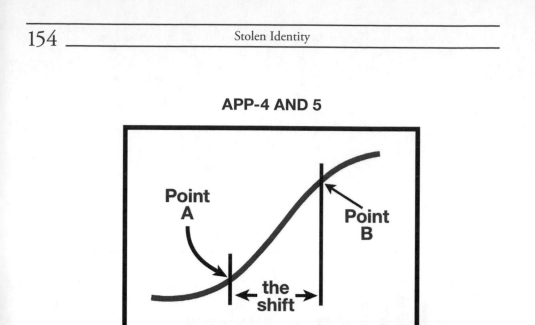

Figure App-4: The shift in many of the events cited is exponential with a Point A and a Point B.

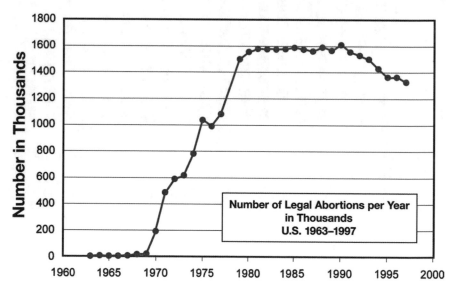

Figure App-5: The number of legal abortions per year in the thousands, United States, 1963–1997. Updated Source: U.S. Census Bureau, Statistical Abstract of the United States: 2012.

From: Hilgers, TW, Blinders: The Destructive Downstream Impact of Contraception, Abortion, and IVF, Beaufort Books, New York, 2018, p. 7

APP-6

Maternal deaths

Women are dying from childbirth at
the highest rate in decades, according
to recent government figures.

Maternal mortality,
per 100,000 live births

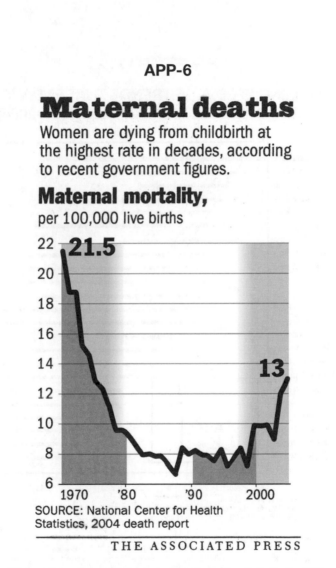

SOURCE: National Center for Health
Statistics, 2004 death report

THE ASSOCIATED PRESS

Figure App-6: Increasing rate of maternal mortality in the U.S.

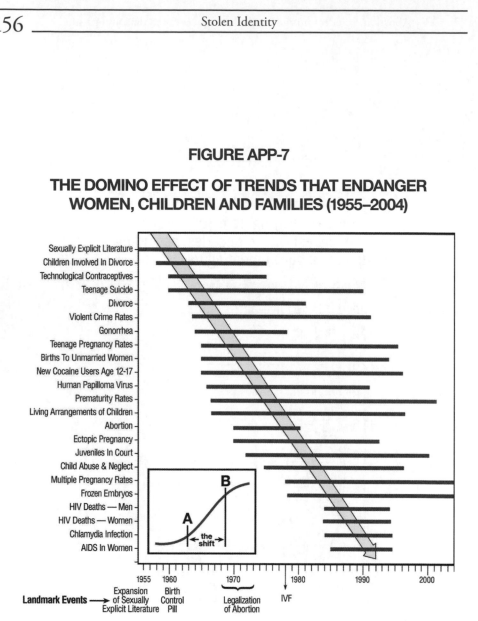

FIGURE APP-7

THE DOMINO EFFECT OF TRENDS THAT ENDANGER WOMEN, CHILDREN AND FAMILIES (1955–2004)

From: Hilgers, TW, Blinders: The Destructive Downstream Impact of Contraception, Abortion, and IVF, Beaufort Books, New York, 2018, p. 70. The length of time the increase in the trend occurred (A to B) and at the level of B, the numbers stayed elevated.

FIGURE APP-8

EACH MEASURED AT THE BEGINNING OF THE EXPONENTIAL RISE (SEE FIGURES APP-4 AND APP-7)

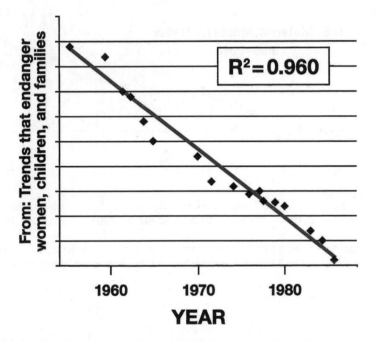

Figure App-8: A regression line establishing a significant linear relationship beginning with point A of the shift. An R² value of 0.960 reveals a statistically highly consistent linear relationship.

From: Hilgers, TW, Blinders: The Destructive Downstream Impact of Contraception, Abortion, and IVF, Beaufort Books, New York, 2018, p. 71.

FIGURE APP-9

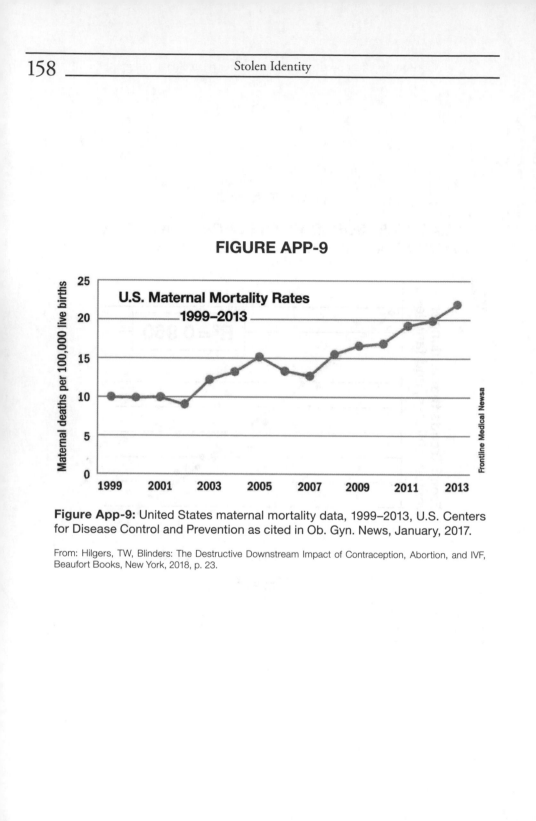

Figure App-9: United States maternal mortality data, 1999–2013, U.S. Centers for Disease Control and Prevention as cited in Ob. Gyn. News, January, 2017.

From: Hilgers, TW, Blinders: The Destructive Downstream Impact of Contraception, Abortion, and IVF, Beaufort Books, New York, 2018, p. 23.

FIGURE APP-10

ABORTION AND TECHNOLOGICAL CONTRACEPTION

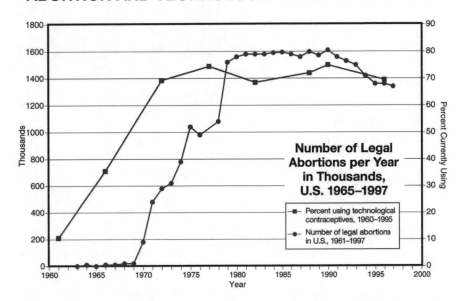

Figure App-10: The number of legal abortions per year in the United States and the percentage of women age 15-44 using technological contraceptives.

From: Hilgers, TW, Blinders: The Destructive Downstream Impact of Contraception, Abortion, and IVF, Beaufort Books, New York, 2018, p. 9.

FIGURE APP-11

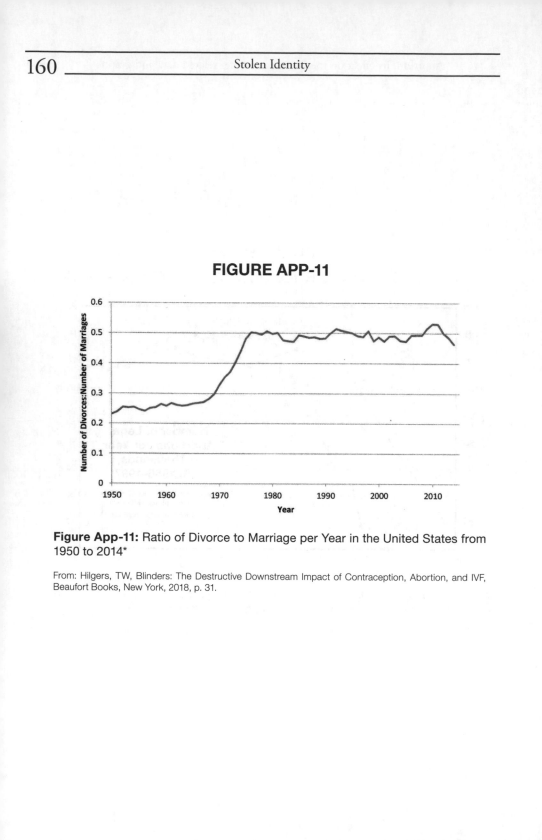

Figure App-11: Ratio of Divorce to Marriage per Year in the United States from 1950 to 2014*

From: Hilgers, TW, Blinders: The Destructive Downstream Impact of Contraception, Abortion, and IVF, Beaufort Books, New York, 2018, p. 31.

FIGURES APP-12 AND 13

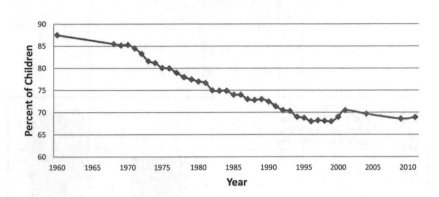

Figure App-12: Percentage of children under 18 living with both biological parents 1960–2011.

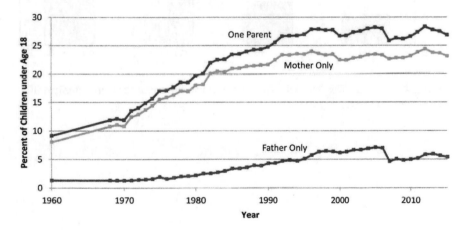

Figure App-13: Living Arrangements of Children Under 18 with One Parent.

From: Hilgers, TW, Blinders: The Destructive Downstream Impact of Contraception, Abortion, and IVF, Beaufort Books, New York, 2018, p. 39.

FIGURE APP-14

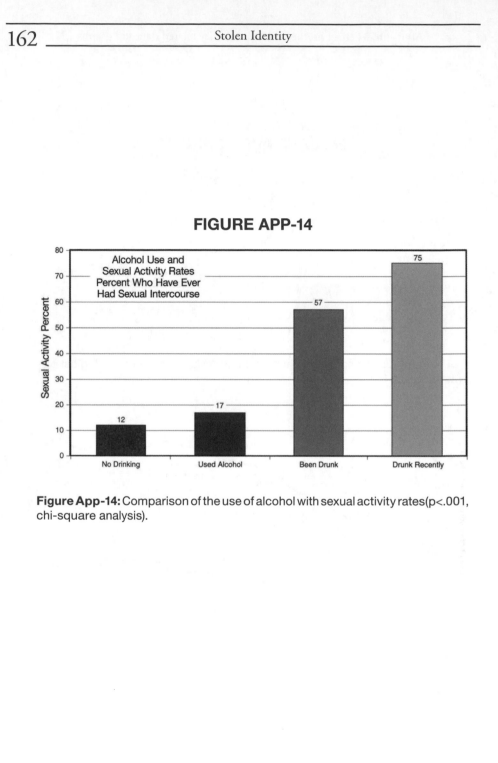

Figure App-14: Comparison of the use of alcohol with sexual activity rates(p<.001, chi-square analysis).

FIGURE APP-15

Figure App-15: The relationship between sexual values and sexual activity rates. The response to the statement. "It is against my values for me to have sex while I am an unmarried teen" compared to involvement in sexual activity. Based on a survey of 1537 students, 15 to 17 years old.

TABLE APP-16

	% men	% women
Straight	96.7	96.6
Gay/Lesbian	1.8	1.4
Bisexual	0.4	0.9
Refused	0.5	0.6
I don't know the answer	0.4	0.4
Something else	0.2	0.2

TOTAL: N = 231,967

Figure App-16: Sexual orientation among adults ages 18 and over by sex: United States 2013[1] Sexual orientation in the 2013 National Health Interview Survey (NHIS): a quality assessment vital health statistics 2(169). 2014 (CDC). (Total n = 231,967).

- The term transgender was not one of the initial responses. In a **follow-up response** to the answer "something else" **5.4 percent of 400** responded as **Transgender**.

- There were 400 respondents that said they were "something else"

- 400 x .054 = **21.6** of 231,967 **were identified as transgender**.

Table 10-3: In the NHIS survey for 2013

From: Hilgers, TW, Blinders: The Destructive Downstream Impact of Contraception, Abortion, and IVF, Beaufort Books, New York, 2018, p. 67.

TABLE APP-17

THE DISTINCTIVE PROBLEMS OF COHABITATING RELATIONSHIPS (WHEN COMPARED TO MARRIAGE)

- Odds of recent infidelity increased more than two-fold.
- Increases the net odds of eventual marital infidelity by 39%.
- Rates of separation were 5 times as high.
- Once separated, they are less likely to reconcile.
- Cohabitants reflect a relatively low level of commitment.
- The children suffer from significantly elevated rates of emotional and behavioral disorders.

Treas J, Giesen D: Sexual Infidelity Among Married and Cohabiting Americans. Journal of Marriage and the Family 62 (2000): 48–60.

Georgina Binstock and Arland Thornton, "Separations, Reconciliations, and Living Apart in Cohabiting and Marital Unions," Journal of Marriage and Family 65 (2003): 432–43.
Scott M. Stanley, Sarah W. Whitton, and Howard J. Markman, "Maybe I Do: Interpersonal Commitments and Premarital or Non marital Cohabitation," Journal of Family Issues 25 (2004): 496–519.
Susan L. Brown, "Family Structure and Child Well-Being: The Significance of Parental Cohabitation," Journal of Marriage and Family 66 (2004): 351–67.

TABLE APP-18

FREEDOMS OF SEXUAL FRIENDSHIP:

- The freedom from unwanted pregnancy
- The freedom from multiple complications of contraception, including its downstream complications
- The freedom from venereal diseases and their bad effects
- The freedom from the complications of abortion
- The freedom from the sorrow that descends upon the family when an unmarried daughter becomes pregnant
- The freedom to explore brained-centered rather than genital-centered sexuality
- The true freedom to embrace both love and life.

---

1. Adapted from: Hilgers TW: The Pregnant Adolescent: A Challenge to the Community. Int Rev Nat Fam Plan, 343-358: 1977.

From: Hilgers, TW, Blinders: The Destructive Downstream Impact of Contraception, Abortion, and IVF, Beaufort Books, New York, 2018, p. 100.

Glossary

-A-

abortion: The termination of a pregnancy either spontaneous or medically or surgically induced, accompanied by, resulting in, or closely followed by the death of the nascent child.

American College (Congress) of Obstetricians & Gynecologists (ACOG): The ACOG is described as the "premier" professional organization for physicians who practice or specialize in obstetrics and gynecology. They were first established in 1951 and are the publishers of the "Green Journal" in Obstetrics & Gynecology. The College often publishes committee opinions and practice recommendations which in a significant way dictates the way obstetrics and gynecology is to be practiced. This poses some difficulties because they're not infallible recommendations, but sometimes are viewed as such because of the medicolegal structure in the United States. It often dictates the way a particular problem should be handled and it is according to the group of physicians (the Committee) who addresses these issues. Often it is their favorite approach to the treatment of a particular problem when in fact other approaches are at least as good, if not better. However, they are the only such organization of its kind. In order to be a member, you must be certified in obstetrics and gynecology and this is done through the completion of an accredited four-year residency program; taking both written and oral Board examinations administered by the American Board of Obstetrics & Gynecology (a separate organization).

Aristotle: (384–322 B.C.) Ancient Greek philosopher and scientist.

-B-

bias: An inclination of temperament or outlook especially a personal and sometimes unreasoned judgment that influences decision making.

Blackmun, Justice Harry: (1908–1999) Harry Andrew Blackmun was an American lawyer and jurist who served as an Associate Justice of the Supreme Court of the United States from 1970 until 1994. Best known as the author of the Court's abortion opinions in *Roe v. Wade* and *Doe v. Bolton*.

-C-

caudal: In a direction toward the buttocks.

Constitution, United States: The United States Constitution (1789) is the supreme law of the United States. The Constitution, originally comprising seven articles, delineates the national frame of government.

contralateral: The opposite side.

-D-

deceptive: Giving an appearance or impression different from the true one; misleading.

Declaration of Geneva: The Declaration of Geneva was adopted by the General Assembly of the World Medical Association at Geneva in 1948, amended in 1968, 1983, 1994, editorially revised in 2005 and 2006 and amended in 2017. It is a declaration of a physician's dedication to the Humanitarian goals of medicine. A declaration that was especially important in view of the medical crimes which had just been committed in German-occupied Europe. The Declaration of Geneva was originally intended as a revision of the Hippocratic Oath as a formulation of that oath's moral truths that could be comprehended and acknowledged in a modern way.

Declaration of Oslo: A statement by the World Medical Association in 1970—amended in 1983—which attempted to modernize the Hippocratic Oath's language on abortions regarding a woman's right to privacy.

dehumanization: To deprive of human qualities, personality, or spirit.

-E-

egg cell: Ovum; a female gamete.

embryo: The developing human individual from the time of implantation to the end of the eighth week after conception.

-F-

fabricated: To make up for the purpose of deception.

fertilization: The process by which the male's sperm unites with the female's oocyte, creating a new life.

fertilized egg: The cell resulting from union of a male and a female gamete: the fertilized ovum; zygote.

fetal age: The age of the conceptus computed from the time elapsed since fertilization or conception.

-G-

Galen: Galen of Pergamon, was a Greek physician, surgeon and philosopher in the Roman Empire.

gestation: The period of development in the uterus until birth counted from the first day of a woman's last menstrual period. This is by its nature wrong by a factor of two weeks. Pregnancy is not 40 weeks, only 38 weeks long.

-H-

Hippocratic Oath: This is an oath historically taken by physicians. It is one of the most widely known of Greek medical texts. In its original form, it requires a new physician to swear to uphold specific ethical standards. The Oath is the earliest expression of medical ethics in the Western world.

Hooker, Davenport, PhD: University of Pittsburgh School of Medicine, a PhD gross anatomist. In January 1939 made film, "Early Fetal Human Activity" which showed fetuses response to outside stimuli in ages 8.5 to 14 weeks gestation.

human being: a man, woman, or child (including the unborn) of the species Homo sapiens.

Hunter, Dr. William: (1718–1783) Anatomist and physician. Wrote a definitive work of his time, "The Anatomy of the Human Gravid Uterus" in 1774 which showed some of the most beautiful drawings of the growth and development of the baby in utero from the very earliest days of development through the time of birth. Was the physician to the Queen.

-I-

Illegal abortion: An abortion performed contrary to the laws regulating abortion. Sometimes referred to as "coat-hanger abortions."

ipsilateral: The same side.

-J-

Johns Hopkins University: The Johns Hopkins University is an American private research university in Baltimore, Maryland. Founded in 1876, the university was named for its first benefactor, the American entrepreneur, abolitionist, and philanthropist Johns Hopkins.

-L-

Lader, Lawrence: (1919–2006) He, along with Dr. Bernard Nathanson, were two of the founders of the pro-abortion group NARAL. Betty Friedan described him as "the founding father of the abortion movement."

Lethalism: the solution of complex social problems by killing the "human problem."

Lethalist: An individual who supports and/or participates in lethal solutions to complex social problems.

ludicrous: So foolish, unreasonable, or out of place as to be amusing; ridiculous.

-M-

maternal mortality rate: Defined as the number of maternal deaths during a given time period per 100,000 live births during the same time period.

-N-

Nathanson, Dr. Bernard: Dr. Nathanson was an original member of the National Association for the Repeal of Abortion Laws (NARAL), was himself an abortionist, but discontinued performing abortions once he learned more about the lives that he was destroying. He was an obstetrician-gynecologist. He became a pro-life activist later in life and produced an ultrasound film called The Silent Scream.

noxious: hurtful; injurious; pernicious.

-O-

obstetrics: That branch of surgery which deals with the management of pregnancy, labor and delivery.

ovaries: The female gonad: sexual glands in which the ova are formed.

ovum: The female reproductive or germ cell which after fertilization is a new member of the same species; called also an egg and sometimes loosely used in reference to the early stages of cellular division prior to implantation.

-P-

phenotype: The outward, visible expression of the hereditary constitution of an organism.

philosophy: The love or pursuit of knowledge and development of thinking.

physician: An authorized practitioner of medicine, as one graduated from a college of medicine or osteopathy and licensed by the appropriate board and licensed by the state.

Planned Parenthood: A non-profit organization that provides birth control in the United States and other countries. It is the largest provider of abortion in America.

Planned Parenthood Federation: Planned Parenthood Federation of America, Inc. (PPFA), formal name of Planned Parenthood. PPFA has its roots in Brooklyn, New York, where Margaret Sanger opened the first birth control clinic in the United States in 1916.

Posterity Clause: In the Preamble of the United States Constitution. The framers wanted this document to contain a most important reaffirmation of the present generation's responsibility to future generations.

prenatal: Existing or occurring before birth.

progesterone: A hormone produced in the ovaries following ovulation and is also produced in large quantities during pregnancy.

Puritanism: An approach to problem solving which is camouflaged in strict approaches to morality, but, in reality, does very little to solve underlying problems.

-Q-

quickening: The first recognizable movements by the mother of the fetus, usually appearing after the 18th week of gestation.

-R-

Relativism: A philosophical approach that sees truth in relation to the group or individual that proposes it. The important feature of relativism is that it sees no moral absolutes. Furthermore, it is not based in an objective judgment of what is morally right or wrong. An action might be considered morally wrong today, but through a subjective assessment, it might be considered morally right tomorrow. The idea that points of view are relative to differences in perception and consideration.

Roe v. Wade: A landmark court decision in the United States issued by the Supreme Court of the United States in 1973 on the issue of the constitutionality of laws that criminalized or restricted access to induced abortion.

-S-

scientific fact: An observation that has been confirmed repeatedly and is accepted as true.

social abortion: The rejection of a pregnant woman by those close to her, such as boyfriend, husband, friends, relatives, physicians, etc. Most induced abortions are preceded by this rejection, placing pressure on the woman to abort the pregnancy due to a lack of support.

sperm cell: The male gamete or sex cell that contains the genetic information to be transmitted by the male.

spermatozoan: The male reproductive cell; the male gamete.

St. Augustine: (354–430 A.D.) St. Augustine of Hippo, Doctor of the Church, bishop, philosopher, theologian.

St. Thomas Aquinas: (1225–1274) An Italian Dominican friar, Catholic priest and Doctor of the Church; an immensely influential philosopher, theologian and jurist.

-T-

testicles: Also called testes or gonads, they are part of the male reproductive system.

-U-

uterus: A hollow muscular organ located in the pelvic cavity of female mammals in which the fertilized egg implants and develops.

Utilitarianism: The ethical theory proposed by Jeremy Bentham and John Stuart Mill that all moral, social or political actions should be directed toward achieving the greatest good for the greatest number of people without any moral absolutes.

-V-

viability: Capability of living; the state of being viable; usually connotes a fetus that has reached 500 g in weight and 20 gestational weeks' development (18 weeks after fertilization). Can also be subdivided into *intracorporeal* and *extracorporeal* viability

-Z-

zygote: The originating cell resulting from the union of a male and a female gamete. Ultimately the initiating cell for all developmental phases and stages of human development that are genetically unique in the growth and development of the human person.

Index

-Q-

-R-

-S-

-T-

-U-

-V-

value of life, 142
viability, 137, 172
violence, 103

-W-

We must know!, 103
with smoothing technology, 63
women, as protector, xii
women's health, 133
words commonly used, 137
www.knowreality.us, 14
www.womanlifechoice.com, 14

-Z-

zygote, human, xiii, 172

Acknowledgments

The author wishes to acknowledge the following individuals in assisting with the work to accomplish the completion of this book. These include the following:

Terri Green: Dr. Hilgers' personal secretary who typed the original manuscript from dictation and made author's corrections after review and editing.

Matthew Johnson: The graphic artist and design professional at the Saint Paul VI Institute who coordinated and completed all of the typesetting and layout for this book.

Angela Adkins-Miller, PhD: Angela was responsible for the proofreading of the completed book and making appropriate editing adjustments where necessary.

The author would like to **thank these three individuals** very sincerely for all of the effort and time that they put into helping complete this book.